GLP-1 High-Protein Cookbook for Beginners

80+ Easy, Muscle-Protecting Recipes for Healthy Weight Loss, Appetite Control & Sustainable Results

John Carter

Table of Contents

Introduction

If you're reading this, you're likely navigating something new - and perhaps confusing.

You've started a GLP-1 medication, like semaglutide or tirzepatide. Your doctor said it would help with weight loss or blood sugar control - and it's working. The scale is moving. But now you're facing something unexpected: you're just not hungry.

Some days, eating feels like a chore. You open the fridge, and nothing appeals. A few bites in, you're full. Nausea and fatigue might set in. Online, you may have seen warnings about muscle loss, nutrient deficiencies, and long-term health risks.

You're caught between two concerns: eating too little and risking muscle loss, or eating more and feeling uncomfortable.

Let me be clear: **you are not broken, and this is not your fault.**

What you're experiencing is a normal reaction to these medications. GLP-1 receptor agonists suppress appetite and slow digestion. That's why they're effective, but it also changes your relationship with food - and no one provided a roadmap.

This book is that roadmap.

What This Book Is Not

This is not another diet book. You won't find calorie-counting, restrictive meal plans, or before-and-after photos meant to make you feel inadequate. You're already eating less - that's the challenge.

This is also not a medical textbook. You won't be overwhelmed with jargon or expected to grasp complex science. You don't need a biology degree to eat well on GLP-1 medication. You need clarity, structure, and practical advice.

What This Book Is

This is a science-backed, real-world guide to nourishing your body while on GLP-1 medication.

It revolves around three core principles:

- **Protein comes first.** With a reduced appetite and calorie intake, muscle loss becomes a risk. Prioritizing protein is the most crucial nutritional strategy you can adopt.

- **Nutrient density over volume.** You can't eat as much as you used to, so every bite must count. This book will teach you to pack nutrition into smaller portions without overwhelm.

- **Structure reduces decision fatigue.** When nothing appeals, an open-ended "what should I eat?" doesn't help. You'll receive clear frameworks, not vague advice.

What You'll Learn

You'll understand why your appetite has changed and what's happening in your body. You'll learn how much protein you need and how to reach that target even without hunger. You'll discover strategies for managing nausea, choosing the right foods, and timing your meals to align with your medication.

You'll also learn how to preserve muscle, support your metabolism, and avoid common pitfalls that make people feel worse.

There are recipes, too. They're straightforward, designed for real life: quick, simple, high-protein, and easy on a sensitive stomach.

A Note on Muscle Loss

If you've researched GLP-1 medications, you've likely seen concerns about muscle loss. It's valid. Research indicates that significant calorie reductions can lead to muscle breakdown, especially if protein intake is inadequate.

But muscle loss is not inevitable.

Experts suggest a minimum protein intake of 1.2 to 1.6 grams per kilogram of body weight to help preserve lean mass during weight loss. Combined with resistance training (even light exercise), this approach significantly mitigates the risk.

You'll find detailed guidance on this throughout the book. Not fear. Not hype. Just clear, evidence-informed strategies.

How to Use This Book

Begin with the foundational chapters. Understand the science in straightforward terms. Then move into the practical sections: meal structure, protein strategies, and recipes.

If you're dealing with nausea or other challenges, jump to the troubleshooting chapters. If you're wondering what to eat today, head straight to the meal plans.

This is a reference guide - use it as needed. Mark pages, highlight sections, revisit it during rough patches.

Who This Book Is For

This book is designed for anyone navigating nutrition while using GLP-1 medication. You might identify with one or more of these categories:

New GLP-1 Users

You've just started semaglutide, tirzepatide, or similar medication. Your appetite has dropped, and you need guidance on what and how much to eat.

Long-Term Users Who Feel Stuck

You've been on GLP-1 for months, maybe longer. Weight loss has plateaued or stopped. You're tired, worried about muscle loss, and need a reset.

Adults Concerned About Muscle Loss

You're aware that rapid weight loss without sufficient protein can lead to muscle breakdown. You want to protect your strength and metabolism.

Busy Professionals

You need uncomplicated, high-protein options that fit into a tight schedule.

Family Members and Caregivers

You're cooking for someone on GLP-1. You want to support them without extra meal prep or uncertainty about what works.

If any of these describe you, this book will be a valuable resource.

One Last Thing

You're undertaking something challenging - changing your body, habits, and health. This requires courage and support.

This book won't solve everything, but it will provide clarity, confidence, and a plan that works with your medication - not against it.

Let's get started.

PART 1
GLP-1 IN 15 MINUTES

Chapter 1:
What GLP-1 Does

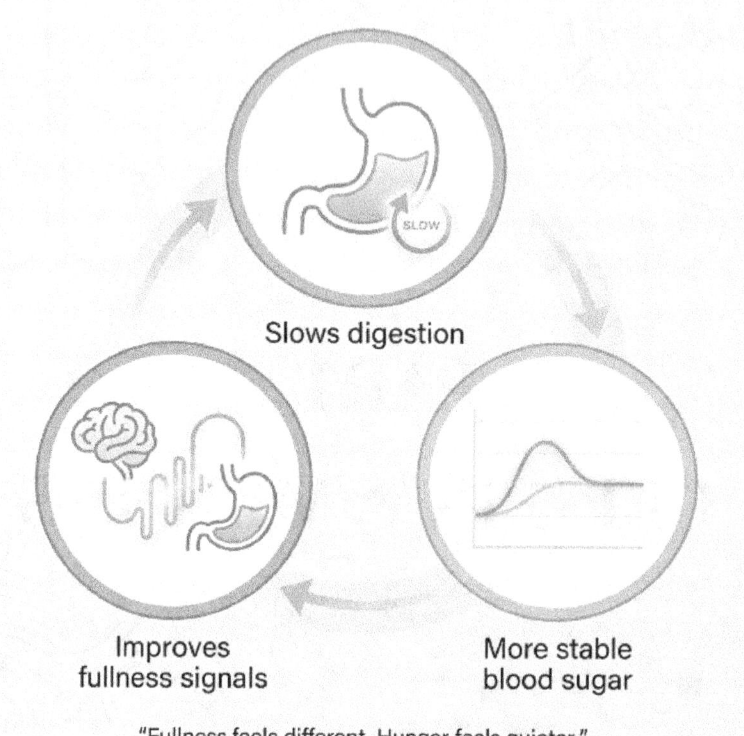

"Fullness feels different. Hunger feels quieter."

GLP-1 medications function uniquely compared to anything you've tried before. They don't merely suppress appetite or increase metabolism. Instead, they fundamentally change how your body processes food, signals hunger, and regulates blood sugar.

Understanding these mechanisms explains why eating feels different on these medications and clarifies why your nutrition strategy must adapt. This chapter outlines the four primary ways GLP-1 impacts your body and what each means for how you eat.

How GLP-1 Slows Digestion

GLP-1 medications delay gastric emptying - the movement of food from your stomach to your small intestine. Normally, your stomach empties within two to four hours after eating. With GLP-1, this process slows significantly.

This delay keeps food in your stomach longer, resulting in prolonged fullness after meals. What once felt like normal satiety now lasts for hours. A moderate breakfast might keep you satisfied until mid-afternoon.

This mechanism also explains common side effects. Nausea, bloating, and discomfort often stem from food lingering in the stomach. Large meals become harder to tolerate, and rich, fatty foods may feel particularly heavy.

What this means for you:

- Smaller, more frequent meals may be more comfortable than traditional portions.
- Eating slowly is essential - your stomach needs time to signal fullness.
- Heavy or greasy foods may trigger nausea more easily.
- Timing matters - eating too close to bedtime can worsen reflux or discomfort.

Slower digestion isn't a side effect to overcome; it's a core mechanism of how these medications work. Adjusting meal size and composition can make the process more comfortable.

How GLP-1 Reduces Hunger

GLP-1 acts on appetite centers in your brain, inhibiting food intake by signaling satiety more strongly and earlier than normal. This isn't willpower; it's a hormonal shift that changes how hunger feels.

Many users find food less interesting. The mental preoccupation with eating diminishes, cravings quiet down, and the drive to snack fades.

Research indicates GLP-1 also alters taste preferences, reducing the appeal of high-fat foods. Foods that once seemed indulgent may now seem unappealing. This shift can reduce calorie-dense choices but might narrow your diet if not managed thoughtfully.

What this means for you:

- You may need to eat by the clock rather than relying on hunger cues.
- Prioritize protein-rich foods even when appetite is low.
- Reduced interest in food can lead to unintentional undereating.
- Taste changes are normal—avoid forcing foods that feel unpleasant.

While appetite suppression is powerful, it comes with risks. When hunger disappears, it's easy to skip meals or eat too little, leading to muscle loss and nutrient deficiencies. Structure becomes more important than intuition.

How GLP-1 Improves Blood Sugar Control

GLP-1 stimulates insulin secretion in response to food intake, helping regulate blood sugar more effectively, especially post-meal. For those with type 2 diabetes, this mechanism can significantly enhance glycemic control.

Even for individuals without diabetes, better blood sugar regulation reduces energy crashes and stabilizes mood. You're less likely to experience post-meal slumps or sudden hunger spikes from blood sugar swings.

This benefit extends beyond weight loss. Clinical experts note that GLP-1 medications show promise for treating heart and kidney diseases, likely due to improved metabolic regulation.

What this means for you:

- Blood sugar stability may reduce cravings and energy dips.
- Balanced meals with protein, fat, and fiber support this effect.
- If you have diabetes, monitor blood sugar closely as medication needs may change.
- Improved metabolic health supports long-term outcomes beyond the scale.

Blood sugar control is one reason these medications differ from traditional weight loss approaches. The hormonal regulation creates a more stable internal environment, making it easier to maintain healthier eating patterns.

Why Fullness Feels Different

Fullness on GLP-1 doesn't resemble normal satiety. It arrives faster, lasts longer, and can feel more intense. Some describe it as hitting a wall - one moment you're fine, the next you're uncomfortably full.

This occurs because GLP-1 slows gut motility and amplifies satiety signals. Your stomach holds food longer, and your brain receives stronger "stop eating" messages, creating a sensation that can feel unfamiliar at first.

For many, this new fullness is initially uncomfortable. It can feel like overeating even when portions are modest. Learning to stop before that wall hits takes practice.

What this means for you:

- Stop eating before feeling full - fullness will catch up.
- Smaller portions prevent the uncomfortable "stuck" feeling.
- Chewing thoroughly and eating slowly helps gauge satiety.
- Overeating, even slightly, can trigger nausea or discomfort.

The intensity of fullness means hunger cues become less reliable. You may not feel hungry even when your body needs fuel. This is why structured eating - planned meals and snacks - is essential for meeting protein and nutrient needs.

Common Mistakes to Avoid

- Skipping meals because you're not hungry. Low appetite doesn't mean low nutritional needs.
- Eating large portions out of habit. Your capacity has changed - adjust accordingly.
- Ignoring protein targets. Appetite suppression makes it easy to undereat protein, increasing muscle loss risk.
- Forcing foods that feel unpleasant. Taste changes are real - find alternatives that work.
- Eating too quickly. Fullness signals are delayed; slow down to avoid discomfort.
- Relying only on hunger cues. Structure your eating around a plan, not just appetite.

Key Takeaways

- GLP-1 slows gastric emptying, keeping food in your stomach longer and extending fullness.
- Appetite suppression reduces hunger and food preoccupation, necessitating intentional meal planning.
- Improved insulin secretion stabilizes blood sugar, reducing cravings and energy crashes.
- Fullness feels different - it arrives faster, lasts longer, and can feel more intense.
- Taste preferences may shift, particularly away from high-fat foods.
- Smaller, protein-focused meals work better than large portions.
- Eating by structure, not hunger alone, prevents undereating and nutrient gaps.
- Understanding these mechanisms helps you adapt your eating strategy for better results and comfort.

Chapter 2:
Why Muscle Protection Matters on GLP-1

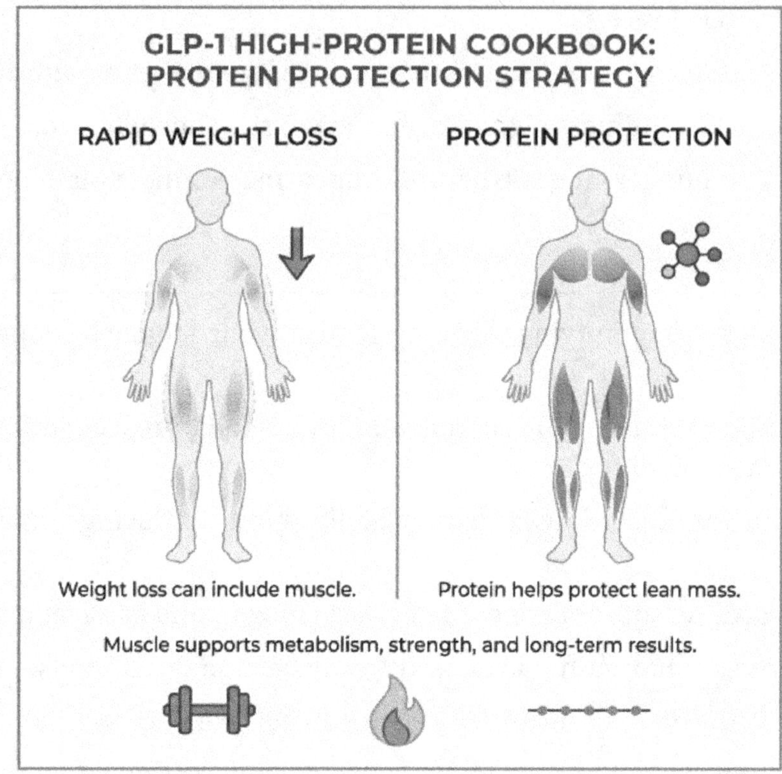

When you lose weight quickly, your body doesn't just burn fat; it also breaks down muscle tissue for energy. This is a significant but often overlooked consequence of GLP-1 medications. How you lose weight matters just as much as how much you lose.

GLP-1 drugs like semaglutide are highly effective, with clinical trials showing an average weight loss of 15%, a remarkable achievement compared to traditional methods. However, research reveals a concerning pattern: between 25% and 39% of the weight lost on GLP-1 medications can come from lean muscle mass. This means that if you lose 30 pounds, up to 12 of those pounds could be muscle.

This chapter explains why muscle loss happens, how to recognize warning signs, and what you can do to protect your muscle while benefiting from GLP-1 therapy.

Why Rapid Weight Loss Risks Muscle Loss

Your body is designed to conserve energy during periods of low food intake. When calorie intake drops sharply - as it often does on GLP-1 medications due to appetite suppression -

your body doesn't distinguish between intentional dieting and starvation. It responds by slowing metabolism and breaking down tissue for fuel.

Muscles require more energy to maintain than fat. So, when your body senses a calorie deficit, especially a steep one, it may prioritize breaking down muscle to reduce its energy needs. This survival mechanism works against your long-term health goals.

GLP-1 medications amplify this risk by effectively reducing appetite. Many users report feeling full after a few bites or forgetting to eat entirely. While this drives weight loss, it also sets the stage for muscle breakdown - particularly if protein intake isn't prioritized.

The faster you lose weight, the greater the proportion of muscle loss. This isn't unique to GLP-1 drugs, but the speed and effectiveness of these medications make muscle preservation a critical focus.

Why Protein Intake Matters

Protein is the building block of muscle tissue. Consuming enough protein provides your body with the raw materials needed to repair and maintain muscle, even in a calorie deficit. Without sufficient protein, your body may break down existing muscle to meet its needs.

On GLP-1 medications, protein becomes even more important. Appetite suppression often leads to lower overall food intake, including protein. If you're eating less but not strategically, muscle loss accelerates.

Research shows that higher protein intake helps preserve lean muscle mass during weight loss. It supports satiety, meaning protein-rich meals can help you feel satisfied even when eating smaller portions. This is especially valuable with an unpredictable appetite.

Protein also has a higher thermic effect than carbohydrates or fats, meaning your body burns more calories digesting it. This supports your metabolism during weight loss and helps counteract the natural metabolic slowdown with calorie restriction.

Basic Daily Protein Targets

How much protein do you need? It depends on your body weight, activity level, and your muscle preservation goals.

General guidelines for GLP-1 users:

- **Minimum target:** 0.7 grams of protein per pound of body weight
- **Optimal target:** 0.8 to 1.0 grams per pound of body weight
- **Active individuals or those prioritizing muscle:** Up to 1.2 grams per pound

For example, if you weigh 180 pounds, aim for 126 to 180 grams of protein per day. If you're highly active or doing resistance training, you may benefit from the higher end of that range.

These targets are higher than standard dietary recommendations because you're in a calorie deficit and using medication that suppresses appetite. You need more protein to counteract muscle breakdown.

Practical protein sources:

- Chicken breast, turkey, lean beef
- Fish and seafood
- Greek yogurt, cottage cheese
- Eggs and egg whites
- Protein shakes or powders (when whole foods aren't enough)
- Tofu, tempeh, edamame

Spread protein intake throughout the day rather than loading it all into one meal. Your body can only use a certain amount of protein at once for muscle synthesis - typically 25 to 40 grams per meal depending on your size and activity level.

Signs You May Not Be Eating Enough

Because GLP-1 medications suppress appetite so effectively, many users unintentionally undereat. This doesn't just risk muscle loss; it can lead to fatigue, nutrient deficiencies, and metabolic slowdown.

Watch for these warning signs:

- **Persistent fatigue or low energy**
- **Weakness during normal activities**
- **Difficulty recovering from workouts** or increased soreness
- **Hair thinning or brittle nails**
- **Feeling cold more often**
- **Loss of strength**
- **Dizziness or lightheadedness**
- **Irregular menstrual cycles** in women

If you're experiencing several of these symptoms, it's a strong indication that your calorie and protein intake are too low. Even though the medication reduces hunger, your body still has baseline nutritional needs.

Track your intake for a few days to get an accurate picture of what you're eating. Many GLP-1 users are surprised to find they're consuming far less protein - and fewer total calories - than they realize.

Combining Protein with Resistance Training

While nutrition is the focus here, protein works best when paired with resistance training. Lifting weights or doing bodyweight exercises signals your body to preserve muscle tissue, even in a calorie deficit.

You don't need to become a bodybuilder. Even two to three sessions per week of basic strength training can significantly improve muscle retention. Some research suggests that combining resistance exercise with higher protein intake can nearly eliminate muscle loss during GLP-1 therapy.

Common Mistakes

- **Relying solely on appetite cues:** Your hunger signals are suppressed—you must eat intentionally.
- **Skipping meals because you're not hungry:** This leads to inadequate protein and calorie intake.
- **Focusing only on the scale:** Weight loss without muscle preservation isn't optimal health.
- **Choosing low-protein "diet" foods:** Prioritize nutrient density over calorie reduction.
- **Not tracking protein intake:** Most people significantly underestimate their protein consumption.

Key Takeaways

- Between 25% and 39% of weight loss on GLP-1 medications can come from muscle, not just fat.
- Rapid weight loss increases the risk of muscle breakdown, especially when protein intake is low.
- Aim for 0.8 to 1.0 grams of protein per pound of body weight daily to preserve muscle.
- Spread protein intake across meals for optimal muscle synthesis.
- Watch for signs of undereating: fatigue, weakness, hair thinning, and feeling cold.
- Pair higher protein intake with resistance training for best results.
- Track your intake - appetite suppression can lead to unintentional undereating.
- Muscle preservation supports long-term metabolic health and sustainable weight maintenance.

Chapter 3:
The 6 Rules of Eating on GLP-1

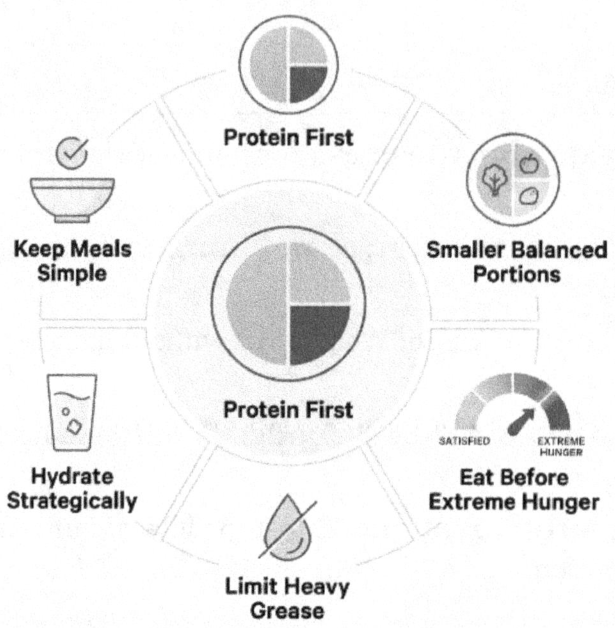

Structure reduces overwhelm. Simplicity protects muscle.

GLP-1 medications adjust how your body perceives hunger and fullness. As your appetite decreases and portions shrink, it's crucial to have a structured eating plan. Without one, you risk muscle loss, nutrient deficiencies, and uncomfortable side effects.

This chapter presents six essential rules to guide your eating while on GLP-1. These are not mere suggestions - they are protective measures to help you lose fat, maintain muscle, and handle the medication's effects on digestion and appetite.

Master these six rules to make eating simpler, safer, and more effective.

Rule 1: Protein First

Why it matters:

GLP-1 can greatly reduce your appetite. Without prioritizing protein, your body may break down muscle to meet its needs.

What to do:

Begin each meal with your protein source - before carbs, vegetables, or any other food. This approach ensures you meet your protein intake even if you can't finish your meal.

Examples:

- Eggs before toast
- Chicken before rice
- Greek yogurt before fruit

Research highlights the importance of protein to prevent muscle loss during GLP-1 treatment. Make it a priority.

Rule 2: Smaller, Balanced Portions

Why it matters:

GLP-1 causes slower stomach emptying. Large meals can lead to nausea and bloating.

What to do:

Use smaller plates and structure meals with protein, carbs, and vegetables. Keep portions about half of what you ate prior to medication.

Practical guide:

- Palm-sized protein
- Fist-sized carb
- Handful of vegetables

Studies show a natural preference for smaller meal sizes. Listen to your body's signals.

Rule 3: Eat Before Extreme Hunger

Why it matters:

GLP-1 blunts hunger cues, risking nutrient deficits and nausea if you wait too long to eat.

What to do:

Eat on a regular schedule, not just when hungry. Set reminders if necessary. Aim for three small meals or four mini-meals, spaced evenly throughout the day.

Warning signs you've waited too long:

- Lightheadedness
- Irritability
- Nausea at the sight of food
- Difficulty finishing even small portions

Structured eating helps prevent over-restriction and maintains nutrient intake.

Rule 4: Limit Heavy Grease

Why it matters:

GLP-1 slows gastric emptying, and high-fat foods can exacerbate nausea and discomfort.

What to do:

Opt for lean proteins and healthier cooking methods like baking, grilling, or air-frying. Use moderate amounts of healthy fats, such as olive oil or avocado, and avoid heavy cream sauces and fried foods.

Better swaps:

- Grilled chicken instead of fried
- Baked salmon instead of breaded fish
- Olive oil drizzle instead of butter-heavy sauces

Managing grease intake helps reduce gastrointestinal symptoms.

Rule 5: Hydrate Strategically

Why it matters:

Excessive water during meals can cause fullness and worsen nausea, yet dehydration is a risk as appetite drops.

What to do:

Sip water between meals rather than during. Maintain consistent hydration throughout the day. If plain water is unappealing, consider herbal tea or sparkling water with lemon.

Timing strategy:

- Hydrate 30 minutes before eating
- Limit fluids during meals
- Resume drinking 30–60 minutes after eating

This approach supports digestion and minimizes discomfort.

Rule 6: Keep Meals Simple

Why it matters:

Complex meals can overwhelm a sensitive stomach. Simplicity helps reduce nausea and makes eating more manageable.

What to do:

Limit meals to 3-5 ingredients and use mild seasonings. Avoid overly spicy, acidic, or sweet dishes if they cause discomfort.

Simple meal examples:

- Grilled chicken, roasted sweet potato, steamed broccoli
- Scrambled eggs, whole-grain toast, sliced avocado
- Baked white fish, quinoa, sautéed spinach

Simple, nutrient-dense meals ensure consistent nutrient intake and minimize deficiencies.

Common Mistakes to Avoid

- **Skipping meals when not hungry** risks muscle loss and nutrient gaps.
- **Forcing large portions** can trigger nausea and deter future meals.
- **Relying on liquid calories** instead of whole foods can reduce satiety and nutrient absorption.
- **Ignoring side effects** like nausea - adjust your diet rather than pushing through.
- **Cutting carbs too low** would affect energy and workout performance; balance is key.

Key Takeaways

- **Protein first, every meal:** It protects muscle and ensures adequate intake despite reduced appetite.
- **Eat smaller, balanced portions:** Follow the three-component plate model: protein, carb, vegetable.
- **Schedule meals before extreme hunger:** Don't wait for hunger cues that may not appear.
- **Limit greasy, heavy foods:** They aggravate nausea and slow digestion.
- **Hydrate between meals, not during:** Strategic timing prevents discomfort.
- **Keep it simple:** Fewer ingredients and milder flavors ensure easier digestion.

These six rules form the foundation for safe and effective eating on GLP-1. Follow them consistently to protect muscle, manage side effects, and support long-term success.

PART 2
THE GLP-1 PLATE SYSTEM

Chapter 4:
The Muscle-Protecting Plate Formula

When you're on GLP-1 medication, every meal becomes an opportunity - not just for weight loss, but for protecting what matters most: your muscle. Research shows that up to 40% of total weight loss can come from lean mass if you're not strategic about what's on your plate. That's the difference between becoming smaller and weaker versus leaner and stronger.

This chapter introduces a simple visual framework: the Muscle-Protecting Plate. It's designed specifically for people using GLP-1 therapy who face reduced appetite, early satiety, and the risk of under-eating protein. You don't need to count every calorie or measure every gram. Instead, you need a repeatable template that prioritizes muscle preservation while working with your medication.

Why Your Plate Composition Matters on GLP-1 Therapy

GLP-1 medications are highly effective at reducing fat mass. Clinical studies confirm they work by slowing gastric emptying, reducing hunger signals, and improving satiety. However, they don't distinguish between fat loss and muscle loss. Your body will break down both unless you provide a reason to hold onto muscle.

That reason is protein - combined with resistance activity and adequate energy intake. When protein intake is insufficient during rapid weight loss, your body turns to muscle tissue for amino acids. This is especially true when calorie restriction becomes too aggressive, which is common among GLP-1 users experiencing significant appetite suppression.

Balanced macronutrient intake supports muscle preservation. Fiber-rich carbohydrates provide sustained energy and improve digestive tolerance, which is critical given the gastrointestinal side effects many users experience. Healthy fats support hormone production and nutrient absorption. But protein is non-negotiable.

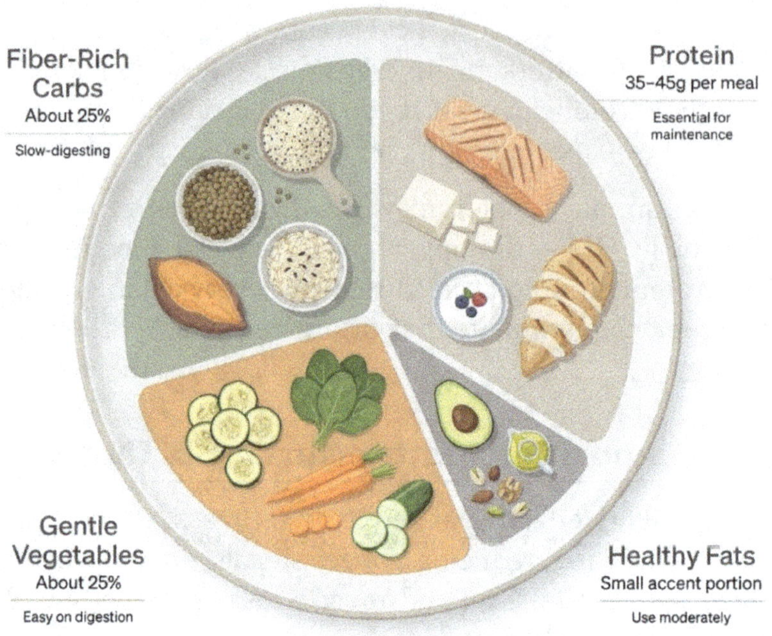

Think of your plate in four sections:

1. Protein (35–45g per meal)

This is your anchor. Protein should take up roughly one-third to one-half of your plate, depending on the meal and your needs.

Why this range? Research suggests adequate protein intake is crucial for muscle preservation during weight loss.

For most people on GLP-1 therapy, aiming for 35–45g per meal across three meals provides a strong foundation. If you're eating smaller, more frequent meals, adjust - but don't skip protein.

Examples:

- 5–6 oz cooked chicken breast
- 6 oz salmon or white fish
- 1.5 cups Greek yogurt
- 2 eggs plus 4 oz turkey sausage
- 6 oz extra-firm tofu with edamame

2. Fiber-Rich Carbohydrates

Carbs aren't the enemy. Fiber-rich options support digestion, enhance the effectiveness of GLP-1 therapy, and provide energy without spiking blood sugar.

Choose:

- Quinoa, farro, or wild rice
- Sweet potato or roasted butternut squash
- Lentils or black beans
- Oats or high-fiber bread

Portion: roughly one-quarter of your plate, or about ½ to ¾ cup cooked.

Fiber also helps with gastrointestinal comfort, a common challenge for GLP-1 users. Pairing fiber with adequate hydration can reduce bloating and constipation.

3. Gentle Vegetables

Vegetables add volume, micronutrients, and additional fiber - but choose wisely. Some raw or cruciferous vegetables can worsen nausea or bloating.

Best options:

- Steamed or roasted zucchini, carrots, or green beans
- Sautéed spinach or bok choy
- Roasted bell peppers
- Cooked asparagus

Avoid or limit:

- Raw broccoli or cauliflower
- Large salads on an empty stomach
- Anything that historically causes gas or discomfort

Portion: fill the remaining quarter of your plate, or more if tolerated.

4. Healthy Fats (In Moderation)

Fats slow digestion further, which can be helpful or problematic depending on your tolerance. Use them strategically.

Examples:

- 1 tbsp olive oil or avocado oil for cooking
- ¼ avocado
- Small handful of nuts or seeds
- 1–2 tsp nut butter

Fats support nutrient absorption and hormone health, but too much can trigger nausea or delayed gastric emptying. Start small and adjust based on how you feel.

Adjusting the Formula When Appetite Is Low

Some days, a full plate feels impossible. That's normal on GLP-1 therapy. When appetite is suppressed:

Prioritize protein first. If you can only eat half a meal, ensure that half includes your protein serving.

Choose calorie-dense proteins. Salmon, Greek yogurt, and eggs deliver more nutrition per bite than chicken breast or white fish.

Sip, don't chug. Protein shakes can help, but drink them slowly to avoid nausea.

Split meals. Eat smaller portions more frequently rather than forcing three large meals.

Don't skip meals entirely. Consistent intake - even small amounts - signals your body to preserve muscle.

Why This Formula Protects Muscle

Clinical experts emphasize balanced intake of fiber, protein, and healthy fats to support muscle mass during GLP-1 therapy. Muscle preservation requires more than just protein - it requires adequate total energy intake. Severe calorie restriction, even with high protein, can still result in muscle breakdown.

The Muscle-Protecting Plate ensures:

- Sufficient protein for muscle protein synthesis
- Enough total calories to prevent excessive metabolic slowdown
- Fiber to support gut health and medication tolerance
- Nutrient density to avoid deficiencies during rapid weight loss

Some studies suggest that combination therapies may improve muscle preservation outcomes, but dietary strategy remains the most accessible and controllable factor.

Common Mistakes

- **Skipping meals because you're "not hungry."** Appetite suppression doesn't mean your body doesn't need fuel.
- **Filling up on vegetables first.** Eat protein before volume foods.
- **Choosing only lean proteins.** Some fat is beneficial - salmon and eggs are better choices than plain chicken breast every meal.
- **Ignoring portion sizes for fats.** A little goes a long way; too much can cause discomfort.

- **Eating the same meals daily without monitoring results.** Track your energy, strength, and how clothes fit - not just the scale.

Key Takeaways

- Structure every meal around 35-45g of protein to protect muscle mass during weight loss.
- Include fiber-rich carbohydrates to support digestion and enhance GLP-1 therapy effectiveness.
- Choose gentle, cooked vegetables over raw or gas-producing options.
- Use healthy fats in moderation to support nutrient absorption without triggering nausea.
- Prioritize protein first when appetite is low - never skip it entirely.
- Adjust portions based on tolerance, but maintain meal consistency.
- Monitor muscle mass and strength alongside weight loss for comprehensive health outcomes.
- Remember: up to 40% of weight loss can be muscle if nutrition isn't strategic.

Chapter 5:
Hitting Your Daily Protein Goal

If you're on a GLP-1 medication, protein isn't optional - it's your primary defense against muscle loss. Suppressed appetite and a smaller stomach can make meeting protein goals feel challenging.

This chapter simplifies the process by detailing how much protein to aim for, illustrating a day's intake at various targets, and offering practical tips to boost protein without resorting to monotonous meals. The aim is to provide clear guidance so you know what to eat, when, and how much.

Why Your Protein Target Matters

GLP-1 medications promote significant weight loss, but without adequate protein and resistance training, some of that weight could be muscle. Research indicates that weight loss via GLP-1 receptor agonists may include undesirable lean mass loss if dietary protein isn't prioritized.

Higher-than-average protein intake helps mitigate this risk.

Your body needs protein to:

- Repair and maintain muscle tissue
- Support metabolic function
- Preserve strength during calorie deficits
- Enhance recovery after resistance training

Appetite suppression reduces spontaneous protein intake, making intentional planning essential.

Reminder - How Much Protein Do You Need?

Most GLP-1 users should aim for **0.7 to 1.0 grams of protein per pound of goal body weight**. This is higher than general guidelines due to increased muscle preservation needs during rapid weight loss.

Example targets:

- Goal weight 130 lbs: **90-130g protein/day**
- Goal weight 150 lbs: **105-150g protein/day**
- Goal weight 180 lbs: **125-180g protein/day**

Begin at the lower end if you're new to tracking, and gradually increase as your tolerance allows. If gastrointestinal side effects are problematic, focus on consistently meeting the minimum.

Sample 90g Protein Day

Breakfast (25g protein)

- 2 scrambled eggs
- 1 slice whole grain toast with 2 tbsp peanut butter
- ½ cup Greek yogurt

Lunch (30g protein)

- Grilled chicken salad: 4 oz chicken breast, mixed greens, cherry tomatoes, olive oil dressing
- 1 small apple

Snack (10g protein)

- 1 oz almonds

Dinner (25g protein)

- 4 oz baked salmon
- 1 cup steamed broccoli
- ½ cup quinoa

Total: 90g protein

This meal structure spreads protein across the day for easier digestion and absorption. Consuming protein post-exercise - within 30 to 60 minutes - enhances muscle recovery.

Sample 110g Protein Day

Breakfast (30g protein)

- Protein smoothie: 1 scoop whey protein, 1 cup unsweetened almond milk, ½ banana, 1 tbsp almond butter

Lunch (35g protein)

- Turkey wrap: 5 oz deli turkey, whole wheat tortilla, lettuce, mustard
- 1 string cheese

Snack (15g protein)

- ½ cup cottage cheese with cucumber slices

Dinner (30g protein)

- 5 oz lean ground beef (93/7) in lettuce wraps
- Side salad with balsamic vinegar

Total: 110g protein

This plan uses convenient, portable options. If nausea is an issue, cold proteins like turkey and cottage cheese are often better tolerated.

Sample 130g Protein Day

Breakfast (35g protein)

- 3-egg omelet with spinach and feta
- 1 slice whole grain toast
- ½ cup Greek yogurt

Lunch (40g protein)

- 6 oz grilled chicken breast
- 1 cup roasted Brussels sprouts
- ½ sweet potato

Snack (20g protein)

- Protein bar (20g+ protein, low sugar)

Dinner (35g protein)

- 6 oz white fish (cod or tilapia)
- 1 cup steamed green beans
- ½ cup wild rice

Total: 130g protein

This structure benefits active individuals or those aiming for higher muscle preservation. Distribute intake evenly to avoid overwhelming your digestion.

Easy Protein Boosters

If you're falling short, these add-ons require minimal effort:

Add to meals:

- 1 scoop protein powder in oatmeal or smoothies: **+20–25g**
- 2 tbsp nutritional yeast on vegetables or salad: **+8g**
- ¼ cup cottage cheese mixed into scrambled eggs: **+7g**
- 1 oz shredded cheese on salad or wraps: **+7g**
- 2 tbsp hemp seeds in yogurt or oatmeal: **+6g**

Standalone snacks:

- 1 hard-boiled egg: **+6g**
- 1 string cheese: **+6g**
- 1 oz beef jerky: **+9g**
- ½ cup edamame: +**9g**
- 1 cup bone broth: **+10g**

Liquid options (for low appetite days):

- Protein shake with water or unsweetened almond milk: **+20-30g**
- Fairlife protein milk (11.5 oz): **+30g**
- Orgain protein shake (ready-to-drink): **+20g**

Liquid protein is often easier to consume when solid food feels overwhelming.

Timing Your Protein

While total daily intake is crucial, timing can enhance results:

- **Post-workout:** Eat 20–30g of protein within 30–60 minutes after resistance training to support recovery.
- **Spread evenly:** Aim for 20–40g per meal, avoiding overly large portions in one sitting.
- **Before bed (optional):** A small protein-rich snack (e.g., Greek yogurt) may support overnight muscle repair.

If nausea is worse in the morning, shift more protein to lunch and dinner.

Common Mistakes

- **Relying solely on shakes:** Whole foods provide additional nutrients and satiety.
- **Skipping breakfast protein:** This can set a low-protein tone for the day.
- **Eating all protein at dinner:** Your body can only utilize so much at once.
- **Choosing low-quality protein bars:** Many are high in sugar and low in protein.
- **Ignoring liquid options:** Drinkable protein is practical when appetite is low.
- **Not tracking:** Estimating often leads to undershooting by 20–30g daily.

Key Takeaways

- **Aim for 0.7–1.0g protein per pound of goal body weight** to preserve muscle during GLP-1 treatment.
- **Spread protein across meals** for better absorption and tolerance.
- **Use sample day plans** as templates—adjust portions to fit your target.
- **Incorporate easy boosters** like protein powder and Greek yogurt when whole meals feel overwhelming.
- **Prioritize post-workout protein** within 30–60 minutes of resistance training.
- **Track your intake** for at least two weeks to establish consistent habits.
- **Choose liquid protein** on low-appetite days to meet minimums without forcing solid food.
- **Combine protein intake with strength training** to signal your body to retain muscle.

PART 3
30-DAY STRUCTURED EATING PLAN

Chapter 6:
First 14 Days – Stabilize & Adapt

The first two weeks on GLP-1 medication lay the foundation for everything that follows. Your body is adjusting to delayed gastric emptying and reduced appetite signals. The aim here isn't perfection - it's about establishing a sustainable rhythm that protects muscle mass while your medication takes effect.

This chapter provides a structured 14-day framework designed to minimize nausea, build consistent protein habits, and reduce decision fatigue. You'll learn what to eat, when to shop, and how to prepare meals efficiently during this crucial adaptation period.

Why the First 14 Days Matter

GLP-1 medications begin working immediately. Appetite suppression and delayed gastric emptying create a narrow eating window where food tolerance can vary daily. Clinical trials show that patients who establish protein-focused eating patterns early maintain significantly more lean tissue during weight loss compared to those who eat less indiscriminately.

The challenge: reduced appetite makes it tempting to skip meals or choose low-protein options. Research indicates that caloric intake often drops sharply with GLP-1 use, potentially below levels needed to preserve muscle mass without a focus on protein.

These first 14 days teach your body a new pattern. You'll learn to eat protein first, recognize true hunger versus medication-induced fullness, and identify foods that settle well.

The Core Principles

Protein comes first, always. With reduced stomach capacity, every bite counts. Aim for 25–35 grams of protein per meal to support muscle preservation as total calorie intake decreases.

Eat smaller, more frequent meals. Delayed gastric emptying means large meals may trigger nausea. Three smaller meals plus one protein-focused snack is preferable to traditional portion sizes.

Choose easily digestible proteins. Your stomach empties more slowly now. Lean proteins like chicken breast, white fish, Greek yogurt, and egg whites digest more comfortably than fatty cuts or heavy casseroles.

Avoid trigger foods initially. High-fat, high-fiber, and spicy foods can worsen nausea during the adaptation phase. Reintroduce these later; the first week isn't the time to test limits.

14-Day Meal Framework

This plan provides structure without rigidity. Each day follows the same pattern: protein-focused breakfast, light lunch, early dinner, and an optional evening protein snack. Adjust portions based on tolerance, but maintain a focus on protein.

Week 1: Establish the Baseline

Days 1–3: Ultra-Simple Proteins

- **Breakfast:** 2 scrambled eggs + 1 slice whole-grain toast
- **Lunch:** 4 oz grilled chicken breast + ½ cup white rice + steamed carrots
- **Dinner:** 5 oz baked cod + small baked potato + green beans
- **Snack:** 1 cup low-fat Greek yogurt

Daily Protein Total: ~110g

These first three days use universally tolerated proteins. No complex seasonings, no heavy sauces. You're establishing that you can consume adequate protein without triggering nausea.

Days 4–7: Add Variety

- **Breakfast:** Protein smoothie (1 scoop whey protein + ½ banana + almond milk)
- **Lunch:** Turkey and cheese roll-ups (4 oz deli turkey) + apple slices
- **Dinner:** 4 oz lean ground turkey + marinara + zucchini noodles
- **Snack:** 2 hard-boiled eggs

Daily Protein Total: ~105g

By day four, most report improved tolerance. This phase introduces different protein sources and textures while maintaining digestibility.

Week 2: Build Confidence

Days 8–10: Structured Flexibility

- **Breakfast:** Cottage cheese bowl (1 cup low-fat cottage cheese + berries)
- **Lunch:** Tuna salad (5 oz tuna + light mayo) on lettuce wraps
- **Dinner:** 5 oz pork tenderloin + roasted Brussels sprouts + quinoa
- **Snack:** String cheese + small handful almonds

Daily Protein Total: ~115g

Week two focuses on increasing meal-prep efficiency. These proteins work well in batch cooking and store safely for several days.

Days 11–14: Real-World Application

- **Breakfast:** Egg white omelet (4 egg whites + vegetables + 1 oz cheese)
- **Lunch:** Rotisserie chicken (5 oz) + mixed greens + balsamic vinegar
- **Dinner:** 6 oz shrimp stir-fry + snap peas + cauliflower rice
- **Snack:** Protein bar (20g+ protein, low sugar)

Daily Protein Total: ~120g

By day 11, you're choosing restaurant-friendly options and convenience proteins, preparing you for sustainable long-term habits beyond the structured plan.

Weekly Grocery Lists

Week 1 Shopping List

Proteins:

- 18 eggs
- 1.5 lbs chicken breast
- 1.5 lbs cod or tilapia
- 1 lb lean ground turkey
- 6 oz deli turkey
- 32 oz low-fat Greek yogurt

Carbohydrates:

- Whole-grain bread
- White rice
- Small potatoes
- Zucchini (for noodles)

Produce:

- Carrots
- Green beans
- Apples
- Bananas

Pantry:

- Whey protein powder
- Marinara sauce (low-sugar)
- Almond milk

Week 2 Shopping List

Proteins:

- 16 oz low-fat cottage cheese
- 15 oz canned tuna (in water)
- 1.5 lbs pork tenderloin
- 1 rotisserie chicken
- 1 lb shrimp
- String cheese (6 pieces)
- Protein bars (4 bars)

Carbohydrates:

- Quinoa
- Cauliflower rice (frozen)

Produce:

- Berries (fresh or frozen)
- Brussels sprouts
- Mixed salad greens
- Snap peas
- Lettuce for wraps

Pantry:

- Light mayonnaise
- Balsamic vinegar
- Almonds (small bag)

Batch Prep Strategies

Sunday Prep (2 hours):

- Grill or bake 2 lbs chicken breast
- Hard-boil 12 eggs
- Cook 3 cups rice or quinoa
- Wash and portion vegetables
- Mix tuna salad for three lunches

Wednesday Refresh (30 minutes):

- Bake fish for remaining dinners
- Prep protein smoothie ingredients in bags
- Portion Greek yogurt into containers

Batch cooking reduces daily decisions when appetite is unpredictable. Pre-portioned proteins eliminate "what should I eat?" paralysis that can often lead to skipping meals.

Managing Common First-Week Challenges

Nausea after eating: Reduce portion size by 25%. Eat slowly. Avoid drinking large amounts of liquid with meals.

No appetite at meal times: Eat anyway, even if portions are small. Skipping meals leads to inadequate protein intake and muscle loss. Start with the protein portion.

Food aversions: Certain proteins may seem unappealing. Keep 3–4 protein options available. Texture often matters more than flavor during adaptation.

Constipation: Common with reduced food volume. Increase water intake gradually. Add small amounts of vegetables. Avoid high-fiber supplements initially as they may worsen bloating.

Extreme fullness: Sign you're eating too much too fast. Cut portions in half. Extend meals over 20–30 minutes instead of 10.

What Success Looks Like

By day 14, you should:

- Consistently achieve 100+ grams of protein daily
- Identify 5–7 well-tolerated protein sources
- Experience reduced nausea frequency
- Have established meal timing that works with your schedule
- Feel confident preparing basic high-protein meals

You're not aiming for perfection. Some days will be harder than others. The goal is establishing a repeatable pattern that becomes automatic.

Key Takeaways

- **First 14 days establish your protein foundation** - this determines muscle preservation success.
- **Target 25-35 grams of protein per meal** despite reduced appetite.
- **Choose easily digestible proteins initially** - chicken, fish, eggs, Greek yogurt, lean turkey.
- **Eat smaller, more frequent meals** to accommodate delayed gastric emptying.
- **Batch prep on Sundays** eliminates decision fatigue when appetite is unpredictable.
- **Track daily protein totals** - aim for 100-120 grams minimum.
- **Adjust portions based on tolerance**, but never skip protein entirely.
- **Week two introduces variety** while maintaining the core structure you established in week one.

Chapter 7:
Days 15–30: Build Strength & Variety

You've completed two weeks on GLP-1 medication. Your appetite has adjusted, and you've established a protein routine. Now it's time to expand your options without losing momentum.

This chapter introduces four distinct flavor profiles - Mediterranean, Tex-Mex, Comfort, and Asian-inspired - designed to prevent meal fatigue while maintaining the protein density your body needs.

Each weekly plan supports muscle preservation, manages reduced appetite, and fits into real-world family meals. You'll receive two complete weekly plans, organized grocery lists, and a protein tracking chart to ensure you meet the recommended 1.2–1.6 g/kg/day target that clinical research identifies as critical during rapid weight loss.

The goal: variety without complexity, flavor without compromise, and structure that supports your metabolism.

Why Variety Matters Now

During weeks three and four, many GLP-1 users experience appetite stabilization. Initial nausea often subsides, but hunger remains suppressed. This creates a challenge: eating the same meals repeatedly becomes unappetizing, yet planning new options feels overwhelming.

Flavor rotation solves this. Cycling through distinct cuisines prevents sensory fatigue while maintaining consistent protein intake. Mediterranean meals offer healthy fats and lean fish. Tex-Mex provides bold spices that stimulate appetite. Comfort foods deliver familiarity. Asian-inspired dishes introduce umami depth.

Each style is adapted for GLP-1 users:

- Smaller portions with concentrated nutrition
- Protein-forward construction
- Minimal prep complexity
- Family-friendly modifications

This approach addresses a documented risk: nutrient deficiencies from decreased food intake. By rotating flavors, you're more likely to consume adequate calories and micronutrients across the week.

Protein Density: The Non-Negotiable

Research consistently shows that muscle preservation during GLP-1 therapy depends on protein intake. Clinical trials document lean mass loss when protein consumption falls below recommended levels, even with significant overall weight reduction.

Your target: **1.2–1.6 grams of protein per kilogram of body weight daily.**

For a 180-pound person (82 kg), this means 98–131 grams of protein per day.

Why this matters:

- GLP-1 medications alter energy metabolism in skeletal muscle
- Rapid weight loss increases risk of lean tissue depletion
- Adequate protein supports muscle protein synthesis despite reduced calorie intake
- Protein has higher satiety value, helping you feel satisfied with smaller meals

Each meal plan is constructed to deliver 30–40 grams of protein per main meal, with 15–20 grams from snacks. This distribution supports sustained energy and nutrient utilization throughout the day.

The Four Flavor Profiles

Mediterranean

Core elements:

- Lean fish (salmon, cod)
- Greek yogurt
- Olive oil in controlled portions
- Herbs: oregano, basil, lemon
- Vegetables: tomatoes, cucumbers, peppers

Why it works:

Mediterranean cuisine naturally emphasizes lean protein and healthy fats. The bright, acidic flavors (lemon, vinegar) can help stimulate appetite.

Family-friendly swap:

Replace whole fish with grilled chicken breast using the same herb blends. Kids often prefer familiar proteins with Mediterranean seasonings.

Tex-Mex

Core elements:

- Lean ground turkey or chicken
- Black beans (protein + fiber)
- Spices: cumin, chili powder, paprika
- Fresh salsa and cilantro
- Controlled cheese portions

Why it works:

Bold spices can counteract taste changes some users experience on GLP-1 medication. The combination of animal and plant proteins increases overall protein density without large portions.

Family-friendly swap:

Build taco bars where each person customizes their plate. Offer tortillas for family members; use lettuce wraps for yourself.

Comfort

Core elements:

- Lean ground beef or turkey
- Mashed cauliflower (replacing traditional potatoes)
- Chicken breast in familiar preparations
- Reduced-fat cheese
- Classic seasonings: garlic, onion, black pepper

Why it works:

Comfort foods provide psychological satisfaction, which matters when appetite suppression makes eating feel mechanical.

Family-friendly swap:

Serve traditional sides alongside protein-dense mains. Your plate focuses on the protein and vegetable; family members add their preferred starches.

Asian-Inspired

Core elements:

- Lean proteins: chicken, shrimp, tofu
- Soy sauce, ginger, garlic
- Stir-fry vegetables
- Controlled rice portions or cauliflower rice
- Sesame oil for flavor

Why it works:

Umami-rich ingredients enhance flavor without added calories. Quick-cooking methods preserve nutrients and require minimal prep.

Family-friendly swap:

Prepare larger batches of stir-fry protein and vegetables. Serve over regular rice for family; use cauliflower rice or skip the base for yourself.

Week 3 Meal Plan: Mediterranean & Tex-Mex Rotation

Monday: Mediterranean

Breakfast: Greek yogurt bowl (1 cup nonfat Greek yogurt, ½ cup berries, 2 tbsp almonds)
Protein: 25g

Lunch: Lemon herb chicken with cucumber tomato salad
Protein: 35g

Dinner: Baked cod with roasted vegetables and quinoa (½ cup)
Protein: 32g

Snack: String cheese + 10 almonds
Protein: 10g

Daily Total: ~102g protein

Tuesday: Tex-Mex

Breakfast: Scrambled eggs (3 eggs) with black beans (¼ cup) and salsa
Protein: 28g

Lunch: Turkey taco lettuce wraps (4 oz ground turkey, lettuce, salsa, 2 tbsp cheese)
Protein: 36g

Dinner: Chicken fajita bowl (4 oz chicken, peppers, onions, ¼ cup black beans, small portion guacamole)
Protein: 38g

Snack: Cottage cheese (½ cup) with cucumber slices
Protein: 14g

Daily Total: ~116g protein

Wednesday: Mediterranean

Breakfast: Protein smoothie (1 scoop protein powder, 1 cup unsweetened almond milk, ½ banana, spinach)
Protein: 25g

Lunch: Greek chicken bowl (4 oz chicken, mixed greens, tomatoes, cucumbers, 2 tbsp feta, lemon vinaigrette)
Protein: 37g

Dinner: Shrimp with zucchini noodles and marinara
Protein: 30g

Snack: Hard-boiled eggs (2)
Protein: 12g

Daily Total: ~104g protein

Thursday: Tex-Mex

Breakfast: Breakfast burrito bowl (3 scrambled eggs, 2 oz turkey sausage, salsa, ¼ avocado)
Protein: 32g

Lunch: Chicken tortilla-less soup (4 oz shredded chicken, broth, tomatoes, beans, spices)
Protein: 35g

Dinner: Beef and bean stuffed peppers (4 oz lean ground beef, ¼ cup black beans, pepper, topped with cheese)
Protein: 40g

Snack: Protein bar (20g protein minimum)
Protein: 20g

Daily Total: ~127g protein

Friday: Mediterranean

Breakfast: Egg white omelet (4 whites) with spinach, tomatoes, feta
Protein: 20g

Lunch: Tuna salad (5 oz tuna, mixed greens, olives, tomatoes, olive oil dressing)
Protein: 38g

Dinner: Grilled chicken with roasted eggplant and tzatziki
Protein: 36g

Snack: Greek yogurt (1 cup) with cinnamon
Protein: 20g

Daily Total: ~114g protein

Saturday: Tex-Mex

Breakfast: Huevos rancheros (3 eggs, black beans, salsa, small corn tortilla)
Protein: 28g

Lunch: Chicken and bean burrito bowl (4 oz chicken, ½ cup beans, lettuce, salsa, small amount rice)
Protein: 42g

Dinner: Turkey chili (6 oz ground turkey, beans, tomatoes, spices)
Protein: 45g

Snack: String cheese + turkey jerky
Protein: 15g

Daily Total: ~130g protein

Sunday: Mediterranean

Breakfast: Cottage cheese (1 cup) with sliced tomatoes and basil
Protein: 28g

Lunch: Salmon (5 oz) with Greek salad
Protein: 35g

Dinner: Chicken souvlaki with roasted vegetables
Protein: 38g

Snack: Protein shake
Protein: 25g

Daily Total: ~126g protein

Week 4 Meal Plan: Comfort & Asian-Inspired Rotation

Monday: Comfort

Breakfast: Protein pancakes (made with protein powder, eggs, topped with Greek yogurt)
Protein: 30g

Lunch: Turkey meatloaf (5 oz) with mashed cauliflower
Protein: 35g

Dinner: Baked chicken breast with green beans and small sweet potato
Protein: 38g

Snack: Cottage cheese (½ cup)
Protein: 14g

Daily Total: ~117g protein

Tuesday: Asian-Inspired

Breakfast: Egg drop soup with added chicken (4 oz)

Protein: 32g

Lunch: Teriyaki chicken (4 oz) with stir-fried vegetables
Protein: 36g

Dinner: Shrimp and broccoli stir-fry with cauliflower rice
Protein: 30g

Snack: Edamame (1 cup)
Protein: 18g

Daily Total: ~116g protein

Wednesday: Comfort

Breakfast: Scrambled eggs (3) with turkey sausage (2 links)
Protein: 30g

Lunch: Chicken pot pie filling (no crust) - chicken, vegetables, light cream sauce
Protein: 35g

Dinner: Beef and vegetable stew (lean beef, carrots, celery, broth)
Protein: 40g

Snack: Greek yogurt (1 cup)
Protein: 20g

Daily Total: ~125g protein

Thursday: Asian-Inspired

Breakfast: Tofu scramble (6 oz firm tofu) with vegetables and soy sauce
Protein: 24g

Lunch: Chicken lettuce wraps (5 oz ground chicken, water chestnuts, soy-ginger sauce)
Protein: 38g

Dinner: Miso-glazed salmon (5 oz) with bok choy
Protein: 35g

Snack: Hard-boiled eggs (2)
Protein: 12g

Daily Total: ~109g protein

Friday: Comfort

Breakfast: Breakfast casserole (eggs, turkey sausage, cheese, vegetables)
Protein: 28g

Lunch: Tuna melt on whole grain (open-faced) with tomato soup
Protein: 32g

Dinner: Meatballs (turkey or lean beef) with marinara and zucchini noodles
Protein: 42g

Snack: Protein bar
Protein: 20g

Daily Total: ~122g protein

Saturday: Asian-Inspired

Breakfast: Congee (rice porridge) with shredded chicken (4 oz) and soft-boiled egg
Protein: 35g

Lunch: Beef and broccoli (5 oz lean beef) with small portion brown rice
Protein: 40g

Dinner: Thai basil chicken (4 oz) with vegetables
Protein: 36g

Snack: Cottage cheese with soy sauce and green onions
Protein: 14g

Daily Total: ~125g protein

Sunday: Comfort

Breakfast: Protein waffles with turkey bacon (3 strips)
Protein: 28g

Lunch: Chicken and dumplings (modified – more chicken, fewer dumplings)
Protein: 38g

Dinner: Pot roast (lean beef) with carrots and mashed cauliflower
Protein: 45g

Snack: Greek yogurt parfait
Protein: 18g

Daily Total: ~129g protein

Grocery List: Week 3 (Mediterranean & Tex-Mex)

Proteins

- Chicken breast (3 lbs)
- Ground turkey (2 lbs)
- Lean ground beef (1 lb)
- Cod fillets (1 lb)
- Salmon fillet (10 oz)
- Shrimp (1 lb)
- Tuna (2 cans, 5 oz each)
- Eggs (2 dozen)
- Turkey sausage (1 package)
- Turkey jerky (4 oz)

Dairy

- Nonfat Greek yogurt (4 cups)
- Cottage cheese (2 cups)
- Feta cheese (4 oz)
- Shredded cheese (8 oz)
- String cheese (7 pieces)

Vegetables

- Mixed salad greens (2 containers)
- Cucumbers (4)

- Tomatoes (8)
- Bell peppers (6)
- Onions (3)
- Zucchini (4)
- Eggplant (1)
- Spinach (1 bag)
- Avocados (2)

Pantry

- Black beans (3 cans)
- Quinoa (1 box)
- Almonds (8 oz)
- Olive oil
- Salsa (1 jar)
- Marinara sauce (1 jar)
- Protein powder (1 container)
- Protein bars (7)

Seasonings

- Cumin, chili powder, paprika
- Oregano, basil
- Garlic, fresh and powder
- Lemons (6)
- Cilantro (1 bunch)

Grocery List: Week 4 (Comfort & Asian-Inspired)

Proteins

- Chicken breast (3 lbs)
- Ground turkey (2 lbs)
- Lean ground beef (1.5 lbs)
- Shrimp (1.5 lbs)
- Salmon fillet (10 oz)
- Firm tofu (1 lb)

- Eggs (2 dozen)
- Turkey sausage (1 package)
- Turkey bacon (1 package)

Dairy

- Greek yogurt (3 cups)
- Cottage cheese (2 cups)
- Shredded cheese (4 oz)
- Light cream (1 cup)

Vegetables

- Broccoli (2 heads)
- Bok choy (1 bunch)
- Green beans (1 lb)
- Carrots (2 lbs)
- Celery (1 bunch)
- Cauliflower (2 heads)
- Mixed stir-fry vegetables (2 bags)
- Lettuce (1 head)
- Water chestnuts (1 can)
- Green onions (1 bunch)

Pantry

- Cauliflower rice (2 bags)
- Brown rice (1 bag)
- Sweet potatoes (2)
- Soy sauce
- Miso paste
- Sesame oil
- Ginger (fresh)
- Protein powder
- Protein bars (7)
- Edamame (frozen, 1 bag)

Seasonings

- Garlic (fresh and powder)
- Black pepper
- Onion powder
- Teriyaki sauce (low-sugar)
- Thai basil (fresh)

Protein Tracking Chart

Use this chart to monitor daily intake and ensure you're meeting your target range.

Day	Target (g)	Breakfast	Lunch	Dinner	Snacks	Total	Met Goal?
Mon	98-131						☐
Tue	98-131						☐
Wed	98-131						☐
Thu	98-131						☐
Fri	98-131						☐
Sat	98-131						☐
Sun	98-131						☐

How to use:

1. Calculate your personal target using your current weight in kg × 1.2–1.6
2. Log protein grams after each meal
3. Adjust next day's meals if you're consistently under target
4. Track patterns: which meals are easiest to hit protein goals?

Common Mistakes in Weeks 3–4

Assuming variety means complexity

You don't need elaborate recipes. Simple protein + vegetable + seasoning works. Flavor rotation is about changing spices and cooking methods, not cooking skill.

Skipping meals because appetite is low

GLP-1 suppression can make eating feel optional. It's not. Skipping meals increases the risk of nutrient deficiencies and muscle loss. Set meal alarms if needed.

Not adjusting portions for family members

Your protein needs are different from those not on medication. Don't reduce family portions to match yours; adjust your plate upward in protein density.

Relying on the same protein source daily

Chicken breast every day leads to meal fatigue. Rotate between poultry, fish, beef, and plant proteins to maintain interest and nutrient diversity.

Ignoring GI symptoms

If certain cuisines trigger nausea or discomfort, note it. Asian-inspired meals with ginger may help some users; others find Tex-Mex spices irritating. Adjust accordingly.

Forgetting to prep

Weeks 3–4 often coincide with return to normal routines. Meal prep on Sunday prevents defaulting to low-protein convenience foods mid-week.

Key Takeaways

- **Flavor rotation prevents meal fatigue** while maintaining protein density critical for muscle preservation during GLP-1 therapy.
- **Target 1.2–1.6 g/kg/day protein** to reduce the risk of lean tissue depletion.
- **Four cuisine styles** (Mediterranean, Tex-Mex, Comfort, Asian-inspired) provide structure without requiring advanced cooking skills.
- **Family-friendly modifications** allow you to prepare one base meal with personalized portions and sides.
- **Track protein daily** using the provided chart to ensure consistent intake despite appetite suppression.
- **Grocery lists organized by week** simplify shopping and reduce decision fatigue.
- **Meal timing matters**: distribute protein across breakfast, lunch, dinner, and snacks for sustained energy and nutrient utilization.
- **Adjust for GI symptoms**: if certain flavors or spices trigger discomfort, swap to a different cuisine rotation that day.

Chapter 8:
Low Appetite Week Plan

Some weeks on GLP-1 medication, eating can feel impossible. Nothing sounds appealing, and you're exhausted, yet too full to eat. Cooking or even chewing feels overwhelming.

This is normal. GLP-1 medications are designed to slow digestion and suppress appetite.

However, skipping meals or eating too little risks muscle loss and further drains energy.

This chapter presents a structured 7-day plan for low-appetite weeks. Every meal is simple, quick, and protein-focused. You'll also find liquid protein strategies and 10-minute fallback options for the days when even "easy" feels hard.

The goal isn't perfection. It's about keeping your body fueled when eating feels like a chore.

Why Low Appetite Weeks Happen

GLP-1 medications activate receptors that signal fullness to your brain and slow food movement through your stomach. The result is prolonged fullness and reduced hunger signals.

Clinical trials show these medications can reduce body weight by 5–18%, mainly through appetite suppression. But this mechanism can also make meeting basic nutrition needs, particularly protein, challenging.

When protein intake drops, muscle loss accelerates. Research suggests that without intentional protein prioritization and physical activity, a significant portion of weight lost can be from lean tissue, not just fat.

Low-appetite weeks mean your medication is working, not that you're failing. You still need a plan to protect muscle and maintain energy.

The 7-Day Low Appetite Meal Framework

Each day includes three ultra-simple options. Choose what sounds least unappealing. Rotate as needed. There's no rule against repeating the same meal multiple days in a row.

Day 1: Liquid-Forward Day

- **Option 1:** Protein shake (25–30g protein) blended with frozen berries and spinach
- **Option 2:** Greek yogurt (1 cup) with honey
- **Option 3:** Bone broth (1 cup) with shredded rotisserie chicken

Day 2: Soft & Mild Day

- **Option 1:** Scrambled eggs (2–3 eggs) with cheese
- **Option 2:** Cottage cheese (1 cup) with canned peaches
- **Option 3:** Mashed white beans with olive oil and salt

Day 3: Cold & Easy Day

- **Option 1:** Deli turkey rolled with cheese slices
- **Option 2:** Tuna salad (3 oz tuna, mayo) on crackers or alone
- **Option 3:** Hard-boiled eggs (2–3) with a pinch of salt

Day 4: Repeat Liquid Day

- **Option 1:** Ready-to-drink protein shake (20g+ protein)
- **Option 2:** Smoothie: protein powder, milk, banana, peanut butter
- **Option 3:** Warm miso soup with tofu cubes

Day 5: Comfort Carb + Protein Day

- **Option 1:** Plain pasta with butter, Parmesan, and shredded chicken
- **Option 2:** White rice with a fried egg
- **Option 3:** Oatmeal with milk, topped with protein powder

Day 6: No-Cook Day

- **Option 1:** String cheese (2–3 sticks) and almonds
- **Option 2:** Protein bar (15g+ protein) and milk
- **Option 3:** Smoked salmon (3 oz) on cream cheese

Day 7: Choose-Your-Own Day

Select any three meals from Days 1–6 that worked best.

10-Minute Fallback Options

When even the simple plan feels too much:

- **Protein shake from powder:** Mix with water or milk and shake. (2 minutes)
- **Microwaved scrambled eggs:** Crack 2 eggs in a mug, whisk, microwave 60-90 seconds. (3 minutes)
- **Greek yogurt from the container:** Open and eat. (1 minute)

- **Rotisserie chicken:** Pull off pieces, eat cold or warm. (2 minutes)
- **Cheese and crackers:** Pre-portioned cheese with any cracker. (1 minute)

These provide 15–25g of protein with minimal effort.

Liquid Protein Strategies

When chewing feels impossible, liquids are your primary tool.

Why liquids work:

They're easier to tolerate when you feel full, move faster through your system, and can deliver significant protein in small volumes.

Best liquid protein sources:

- **Protein shakes:** Aim for 20–30g protein per serving. Choose ready-to-drink for zero-prep days.
- **Greek yogurt drinks:** 12–15g protein per bottle.
- **Bone broth with protein powder:** Whisk in unflavored collagen or protein powder.
- **Milk-based smoothies:** Blend whole milk or high-protein alternatives with protein powder and frozen fruit.
- **Protein-fortified soups:** Add protein powder to tomato or pureed vegetable soups.

Sipping strategy:

Don't rush a full shake. Sip over 30–60 minutes. Frequent, small intakes are easier than large volumes at once.

Muscle Preservation During Low Appetite Weeks

Low appetite doesn't stop muscle loss. Your body still needs protein to maintain lean tissue.

Minimum daily protein target:

Aim for 60–80g per day, spread over small portions. This is lower than ideal but serves as a protective floor.

Protein-first rule:

When eating, start with the protein portion. Eat the eggs before the toast. Drink the shake first. This ensures baseline needs are met, even if the meal isn't finished.

Pair with light movement:

Even a 10-minute walk or a few squats signal your body to preserve muscle. Just enough movement reminds your muscles they're still needed.

Common Mistakes During Low Appetite Weeks

- **Skipping meals entirely:** Increases muscle loss and fatigue.
- **Relying only on carbs:** Carbs like toast are easy, but don't protect muscle.
- **Waiting for hunger to return:** Hunger may not come back for days. Eat by the clock, not by appetite.
- **Forcing large portions:** Small, frequent intake is better than big meals.
- **Avoiding all liquids:** Liquid calories and protein are helpful tools.

Key Takeaways

- Low appetite weeks are a normal response to GLP-1 medications.
- Prioritize simple, protein-rich meals that require minimal effort.
- Use liquid protein sources when solid food feels impossible.
- Aim for 60–80g protein daily, spread across small portions.
- Eat protein first, even if you can't finish the rest of the meal.
- Rotate the 7-day plan as needed; repetition is fine.
- Keep 10-minute fallback options on hand for tough days.
- Pair protein intake with light movement to preserve muscle mass.

PART 4
THE RECIPES

Chapter 9:
High-Protein Breakfasts

Breakfast on GLP-1 medication presents a unique challenge. Your appetite may be lowest in the morning, yet this is when your body needs protein most to preserve muscle and sustain energy throughout the day. Skipping breakfast or choosing low-protein options can lead to muscle loss, afternoon energy crashes, and difficulty meeting your daily protein targets.

The solution is strategic, high-protein breakfasts that deliver 20–40g of protein without overwhelming your reduced appetite. These recipes prioritize easily digestible protein sources like eggs and Greek yogurt, which clinical evidence shows are well-tolerated by GLP-1 users. Each recipe is designed to be prepared in under 20 minutes, recognizing that morning nausea or time constraints are common barriers.

High-protein breakfasts enhance satiety, helping you feel satisfied longer while supporting muscle preservation. Research indicates that consuming 25–30g of protein per meal optimizes muscle maintenance during weight loss. These recipes meet or exceed that threshold while incorporating moderate healthy fats for sustained energy and absorption of fat-soluble vitamins.

You'll find egg-based options, yogurt bowls, protein-enhanced smoothies, and light carb combinations. Each recipe includes full nutrition information, substitutions for dietary preferences, and storage guidance for meal prep efficiency.

Classic Protein-Packed Scramble

Why it works: Eggs are one of the most bioavailable protein sources, meaning your body efficiently absorbs and uses the protein. The addition of cottage cheese boosts protein content while creating a creamy texture that's gentle on sensitive stomachs. This combination delivers complete amino acids essential for muscle preservation.

Prep time: 3 minutes

Cook time: 5 minutes

Protein: 32g

Ingredients

- 3 large eggs
- ¼ cup low-fat cottage cheese
- 1 cup spinach, chopped
- 2 tablespoons diced bell pepper
- 1 teaspoon olive oil
- Salt and pepper to taste
- Optional: 1 tablespoon shredded cheese

Instructions

1. Heat olive oil in a non-stick skillet over medium heat.
2. Whisk eggs and cottage cheese together until combined.
3. Add spinach and bell pepper to the skillet, sauté for 1 minute.
4. Pour egg mixture over vegetables, stirring gently.
5. Cook 3–4 minutes, stirring occasionally, until eggs are set but still moist.
6. Season with salt and pepper. Top with shredded cheese if desired.

Nutrition (per serving)

- Calories: 285
- Protein: 32g
- Carbohydrates: 5g
- Fat: 15g
- Fiber: 1g
- Sugar: 3g

Substitutions

- Use egg whites (6) for lower fat
- Swap cottage cheese for ricotta
- Add mushrooms instead of peppers for variety

Storage

Refrigerate up to 3 days. Reheat gently in the microwave for 45 seconds, stirring halfway.

Tip: Slightly undercook eggs before storing—they'll finish cooking when reheated.

Greek Yogurt Protein Bowl

Quick | High Protein | Gentle

Why it works: Greek yogurt provides concentrated protein with probiotics that support digestive health, important when GLP-1 medications slow gastric emptying. The combination of protein and healthy fats from nuts creates sustained energy without blood sugar spikes. This no-cook option is ideal for mornings when nausea makes cooking unappealing.

Prep time: 5 minutes

Cook time: 0 minutes

Protein: 28g

Ingredients

- 1 cup plain non-fat Greek yogurt
- 1 scoop vanilla protein powder (20g protein)
- 2 tablespoons sliced almonds
- ½ cup mixed berries
- 1 teaspoon chia seeds
- Optional: 5 drops liquid stevia or 1 teaspoon honey

Instructions

1. Place Greek yogurt in a bowl.
2. Stir in protein powder until smooth.
3. Top with berries, almonds, and chia seeds.
4. Drizzle with sweetener if desired.
5. Let sit 2 minutes to allow chia seeds to soften slightly.

Nutrition (per serving)

- Calories: 320
- Protein: 28g
- Carbohydrates: 22g
- Fat: 10g
- Fiber: 6g
- Sugar: 12g

Substitutions

- Use plant-based yogurt with added protein
- Replace almonds with walnuts or pumpkin seeds
- Swap berries for diced apple or pear

Storage

Assemble dry ingredients separately; combine with yogurt fresh each morning. Prepared bowl keeps 1 day refrigerated.

Tip: Mix protein powder with 1 tablespoon water first to prevent clumping.

Veggie-Loaded Egg White Frittata

🕐 Quick | ⬭ High Protein | 👫 Family Friendly

Why it works: Egg whites deliver pure protein with minimal fat, reducing the risk of GI discomfort some users experience with whole eggs. Vegetables add fiber and micronutrients without adding significant calories. This recipe makes multiple servings, perfect for meal prep when appetite is unpredictable.

Prep time: 8 minutes

Cook time: 12 minutes

Protein: 24g

Ingredients

- 8 egg whites (or 1 cup liquid egg whites)
- 2 whole eggs
- ½ cup diced zucchini
- ½ cup cherry tomatoes, halved
- ¼ cup diced onion
- ¼ cup reduced-fat feta cheese
- 1 teaspoon olive oil
- ½ teaspoon dried oregano
- Salt and pepper to taste

Instructions

1. Preheat oven to 375°F.
2. Heat olive oil in an oven-safe skillet over medium heat.
3. Sauté zucchini, tomatoes, and onion for 3–4 minutes.
4. Whisk egg whites, whole eggs, oregano, salt, and pepper.
5. Pour egg mixture over vegetables, sprinkle with feta.
6. Cook on stovetop 2 minutes without stirring.
7. Transfer skillet to oven, bake 10 minutes until set.
8. Cut into 4 wedges.

Nutrition (per wedge)

- Calories: 110
- Protein: 24g
- Carbohydrates: 4g
- Fat: 5g
- Fiber: 1g
- Sugar: 2g

Substitutions

- Use whole eggs (6 total) for higher fat version
- Replace feta with goat cheese or omit for dairy-free
- Add bell peppers or asparagus

Storage

Refrigerate wedges up to 5 days. Reheat in microwave 60 seconds or eat cold.

Tip: Line the skillet with parchment for easier removal and cleanup.

Protein Power Smoothie

⏱ Quick | ◯ High Protein | 🥣 Gentle

Why it works: Liquid nutrition is often better tolerated when solid food feels overwhelming. This smoothie delivers complete protein with easily digestible ingredients. The combination of protein powder and Greek yogurt provides 40g of protein in a format that's gentle on the stomach and quick to consume.

Prep time: 5 minutes

Cook time: 0 minutes

Protein: 40g

Ingredients

- 1 scoop vanilla protein powder (25g protein)
- ½ cup plain non-fat Greek yogurt
- 1 cup unsweetened almond milk
- ½ frozen banana
- 1 tablespoon almond butter
- ½ cup ice
- Optional: 1 cup spinach (won't taste it)

Instructions

1. Add almond milk and Greek yogurt to blender.
2. Add protein powder, banana, and almond butter.
3. Add ice and spinach if using.
4. Blend on high 45–60 seconds until smooth.
5. Add more almond milk if too thick.

Nutrition (per serving)

- Calories: 380
- Protein: 40g
- Carbohydrates: 28g
- Fat: 12g
- Fiber: 4g
- Sugar: 14g

Substitutions

- Use any milk (dairy increases protein)
- Replace banana with ½ cup berries
- Swap almond butter for peanut butter or sunflower seed butter

Storage

Best consumed immediately. Can refrigerate up to 8 hours; shake well before drinking.

Tip: Freeze overripe bananas in chunks for perfect smoothie texture.

Cottage Cheese Protein Pancakes

Why it works: These pancakes use cottage cheese and eggs as the base, eliminating most flour and creating a protein-dense breakfast that feels indulgent. The texture is light and fluffy, making them easier to eat when appetite is reduced. Each serving provides muscle-supporting protein without the blood sugar spike of traditional pancakes.

Prep time: 5 minutes

Cook time: 8 minutes

Protein: 28g

Ingredients

- ½ cup low-fat cottage cheese
- 2 large eggs
- ¼ cup oat flour (or blended oats)
- ½ teaspoon vanilla extract
- ½ teaspoon baking powder
- Pinch of cinnamon
- Cooking spray
- Optional: sugar-free syrup for serving

Instructions

1. Blend cottage cheese, eggs, oat flour, vanilla, baking powder, and cinnamon until smooth.
2. Let batter rest 2 minutes to thicken.
3. Heat non-stick skillet over medium heat, spray with cooking spray.
4. Pour ¼ cup batter per pancake.
5. Cook 2–3 minutes until bubbles form, flip and cook 2 minutes more.
6. Makes 4 small pancakes.

Nutrition (per serving, 4 pancakes)

- Calories: 245
- Protein: 28g
- Carbohydrates: 16g
- Fat: 8g
- Fiber: 2g
- Sugar: 4g

Substitutions

- Use almond flour instead of oat flour
- Replace cottage cheese with ricotta
- Add 1 scoop vanilla protein powder for extra protein

Storage

Refrigerate up to 4 days or freeze up to 2 months. Reheat in toaster or microwave.

Tip: Don't overmix—small lumps are fine and create fluffier pancakes.

Smoked Salmon Egg Wrap

⏱ Quick | ◯ High Protein | 🥣 Gentle

Why it works: Smoked salmon provides omega-3 fatty acids and high-quality protein that's easy to digest. The egg wrap eliminates heavy bread, reducing carbohydrate load while maintaining a satisfying handheld format. This combination of protein sources delivers complete amino acids essential for muscle preservation.

Prep time: 5 minutes

Cook time: 4 minutes

Protein: 26g

Ingredients

- 2 large eggs
- 2 oz smoked salmon
- 2 tablespoons light cream cheese
- ¼ cup diced cucumber
- 1 tablespoon diced red onion
- 1 teaspoon fresh dill (or ½ teaspoon dried)
- Cooking spray
- Black pepper to taste

Instructions

1. Whisk eggs with dill and pepper.
2. Heat non-stick skillet over medium-low heat, spray with cooking spray.
3. Pour eggs into skillet, swirl to create thin layer.
4. Cook 2 minutes without stirring until set, flip and cook 1 minute.
5. Transfer egg wrap to plate.
6. Spread cream cheese down the center, top with salmon, cucumber, and onion.
7. Roll tightly and cut in half.

Nutrition (per serving)

- Calories: 265
- Protein: 26g
- Carbohydrates: 5g
- Fat: 15g
- Fiber: 0g
- Sugar: 3g

Substitutions

- Use turkey or chicken breast instead of salmon
- Replace cream cheese with Greek yogurt mixed with herbs
- Add avocado slices for healthy fats

Storage

Best eaten fresh. Assembled wrap keeps 1 day refrigerated; may become slightly soggy.

Tip: Cook egg wrap on lower heat to prevent browning and maintain flexibility for rolling.

Protein-Boosted Oatmeal

⏱ Quick | 🥚 High Protein | 🥣 Gentle | 👨‍👩‍👧 Family Friendly

Why it works: Traditional oatmeal is low in protein, but this version incorporates protein powder and egg whites during cooking, creating a creamy, protein-rich breakfast. Oats provide soluble fiber that supports digestive health, while the protein content keeps you satisfied for hours without the heavy feeling of high-fat options.

Prep time: 2 minutes

Cook time: 6 minutes

Protein: 30g

Ingredients

- ½ cup old-fashioned oats
- 1 cup water
- ¼ cup liquid egg whites
- 1 scoop vanilla protein powder (20g protein)
- 1 tablespoon almond butter
- ½ teaspoon cinnamon
- Pinch of salt
- Optional: ½ sliced banana or berries

Instructions

1. Combine oats, water, and salt in saucepan.
2. Bring to boil, reduce heat to medium-low.
3. Stir in egg whites, cooking and stirring constantly for 2 minutes.
4. Remove from heat, stir in protein powder and cinnamon until smooth.
5. Top with almond butter and fruit if desired.

Nutrition (per serving)

- Calories: 355
- Protein: 30g
- Carbohydrates: 35g
- Fat: 10g
- Fiber: 6g
- Sugar: 3g

Substitutions

- Use steel-cut oats (increase cook time to 15 minutes)
- Replace almond butter with any nut or seed butter
- Use unflavored protein powder and add vanilla extract

Storage

Refrigerate up to 3 days. Add a splash of water or milk when reheating; microwave 90 seconds.

Tip: Stir egg whites in quickly while cooking to incorporate without scrambling.

Turkey Sausage Breakfast Bowl

⏱ Quick | 🥚 High Protein | 👨‍👩‍👧 Family Friendly

Why it works: Lean turkey sausage provides substantial protein with less fat than pork sausage, reducing the risk of GI discomfort. The combination of protein and vegetables creates a balanced meal that supports muscle preservation while delivering essential micronutrients. This savory option works well for those who don't prefer sweet breakfasts.

Prep time: 5 minutes

Cook time: 12 minutes

Protein: 32g

Ingredients

- 4 oz lean turkey sausage (90% lean or higher)
- 2 large eggs
- 1 cup diced sweet potato
- ½ cup diced bell pepper
- ¼ cup diced onion
- 1 teaspoon olive oil
- ½ teaspoon smoked paprika
- Salt and pepper to taste
- Optional: hot sauce for serving

Instructions

1. Heat olive oil in skillet over medium heat.
2. Add sweet potato, cook for 5 minutes stirring occasionally.
3. Add turkey sausage (removed from casing if links), breaking into crumbles.
4. Add bell pepper and onion, cook 4 minutes until sausage is browned.
5. Push mixture to sides, crack eggs into center.
6. Scramble eggs, then mix with sausage and vegetables.
7. Season with paprika, salt, and pepper.

Nutrition (per serving)

- Calories: 385
- Protein: 32g
- Carbohydrates: 22g
- Fat: 18g
- Fiber: 3g
- Sugar: 6g

Substitutions

- Use chicken sausage or plant-based sausage
- Replace sweet potato with regular potato or cauliflower
- Add spinach or kale in the final minute of cooking

Storage

Refrigerate up to 4 days. Reheat in microwave 90 seconds or on stovetop.

Tip: Pre-cook sweet potato in microwave for 3 minutes to reduce stovetop time.

Protein Chia Pudding

Quick | High Protein | Gentle | Plant-Based

Why it works: Chia pudding is prepared the night before, perfect for mornings when appetite or energy is low. Chia seeds provide fiber and omega-3s, while protein powder boosts the protein content to muscle-supporting levels. The pudding-like texture is gentle on sensitive stomachs and easy to consume in small portions.

Prep time: 5 minutes (plus overnight setting)

Cook time: 0 minutes

Protein: 26g

Ingredients

- 1 cup unsweetened almond milk
- 1 scoop vanilla protein powder (20g protein)
- 3 tablespoons chia seeds
- ½ teaspoon vanilla extract
- Optional: 5 drops liquid stevia
- Toppings: ¼ cup berries, 1 tablespoon sliced almonds

Instructions

1. Whisk almond milk and protein powder until smooth.
2. Stir in chia seeds and vanilla extract.
3. Add sweetener if desired.
4. Pour into jar or container, cover, and refrigerate overnight (minimum 4 hours).
5. Stir before serving, add toppings.

Nutrition (per serving)

- Calories: 280
- Protein: 26g
- Carbohydrates: 20g
- Fat: 12g
- Fiber: 12g
- Sugar: 2g

Substitutions

- Use any milk (dairy increases protein)
- Replace chia seeds with ground flaxseed (reduce to 2 tablespoons)
- Try chocolate protein powder with cocoa nibs

Storage

Refrigerate up to 5 days. Stir before eating; add liquid if too thick.

Tip: Make 3–4 servings at once in individual jars for grab-and-go convenience.

Egg Muffin Cups

◯ High Protein | 👪 Family Friendly

Why it works: These portable egg cups are ideal for meal prep and portion control. Each muffin delivers concentrated protein in a format that's easy to eat even with reduced appetite. The vegetables add nutrients and fiber without adding significant calories, and the individual portions prevent overeating.

Prep time: 10 minutes

Cook time: 18 minutes

Protein: 20g (per 2 muffins)

Ingredients (makes 12 muffins)

- 8 large eggs
- ¼ cup milk (any type)
- 1 cup diced ham or turkey
- ½ cup shredded reduced-fat cheese
- 1 cup chopped spinach
- ½ cup diced bell pepper
- ¼ teaspoon garlic powder
- Salt and pepper to taste
- Cooking spray

Instructions

1. Preheat oven to 350°F. Spray muffin tin with cooking spray.
2. Whisk eggs, milk, garlic powder, salt, and pepper.
3. Divide ham, cheese, spinach, and bell pepper among 12 muffin cups.
4. Pour egg mixture over fillings, filling each cup ¾ full.
5. Bake 18–20 minutes until eggs are set and tops are lightly golden.
6. Cool 5 minutes before removing from tin.

Nutrition (per 2 muffins)

- Calories: 210
- Protein: 20g
- Carbohydrates: 3g
- Fat: 12g
- Fiber: 1g
- Sugar: 2g

Substitutions

- Use egg whites only for lower fat
- Replace ham with cooked sausage or bacon
- Add mushrooms, tomatoes, or zucchini

Storage

Refrigerate up to 5 days or freeze up to 3 months. Reheat from frozen in microwave 60–90 seconds.

Tip: Use silicone muffin cups for easiest removal and cleanup.

Protein-Packed Breakfast Burrito

⏱ Quick | ⬭ High Protein | 👫 Family Friendly

Why it works: This burrito uses a high-protein tortilla to boost protein content while maintaining a familiar breakfast format. The combination of eggs, beans, and cheese provides complete protein with fiber for sustained energy. It's portable and can be prepared in advance for busy mornings.

Prep time: 5 minutes

Cook time: 8 minutes

Protein: 35g

Ingredients

- 1 high-protein tortilla (10" size, 12g+ protein)
- 3 large eggs
- ¼ cup black beans, drained and rinsed
- 2 tablespoons shredded reduced-fat cheddar
- 2 tablespoons salsa
- 1 tablespoon diced green chilies
- Cooking spray
- Optional: 1 tablespoon Greek yogurt

Instructions

1. Spray skillet with cooking spray, heat over medium.
2. Whisk eggs, pour into skillet.
3. Scramble eggs until just set, about 3 minutes.
4. Warm tortilla in microwave 15 seconds.
5. Layer eggs, beans, cheese, salsa, and chilies down center of tortilla.
6. Fold sides in, roll tightly.
7. Optional: return to skillet to crisp exterior, 1 minute per side.

Nutrition (per serving)

- Calories: 420
- Protein: 35g
- Carbohydrates: 35g
- Fat: 16g
- Fiber: 12g
- Sugar: 3g

Substitutions

- Use regular tortilla (reduce protein to 28g)
- Replace black beans with pinto beans
- Add cooked turkey sausage for extra protein

Storage

Wrap tightly in foil, refrigerate up to 3 days or freeze up to 2 months. Reheat in microwave 90 seconds or oven at 350°F for 15 minutes.

Tip: Slightly undercook eggs before storing—they'll finish when reheated.

Ricotta Berry Bowl

⏱ Quick | ◯ High Protein | 🥣 Gentle

Why it works: Ricotta cheese provides concentrated protein with a creamy texture that's easy to eat when appetite is low. The mild flavor is gentle on sensitive stomachs, and the combination of protein and antioxidant-rich berries supports both muscle preservation and overall health. This no-cook option requires minimal effort.

Prep time: 4 minutes

Cook time: 0 minutes

Protein: 24g

Ingredients

- ¾ cup part-skim ricotta cheese
- ½ scoop vanilla protein powder (10g protein)
- ½ cup mixed berries
- 1 tablespoon sliced almonds
- 1 teaspoon honey
- ½ teaspoon vanilla extract
- Pinch of cinnamon

Instructions

1. Mix ricotta, protein powder, vanilla extract, and cinnamon until smooth.
2. Transfer to bowl.
3. Top with berries and almonds.
4. Drizzle with honey.

Nutrition (per serving)

- Calories: 310
- Protein: 24g
- Carbohydrates: 25g
- Fat: 12g
- Fiber: 4g
- Sugar: 16g

Substitutions

- Use cottage cheese instead of ricotta
- Replace berries with diced peach or apple
- Swap almonds for walnuts or pecans

Storage

Mix ricotta and protein powder up to 2 days ahead. Add toppings fresh before eating.

Tip: Let ricotta sit at room temperature 10 minutes for creamier texture.

Spinach Feta Egg Bake

◯ High Protein | 👪 Family Friendly

Why it works: This crustless quiche-style dish delivers high protein with vegetables and calcium-rich feta cheese. The absence of a crust reduces carbohydrates and calories while maintaining a satisfying texture. It's ideal for meal prep, providing multiple protein-rich servings throughout the week.

Prep time: 8 minutes

Cook time: 25 minutes

Protein: 22g (per serving, serves 4)

Ingredients

- 8 large eggs
- ½ cup milk (any type)
- 2 cups fresh spinach, chopped
- ½ cup crumbled feta cheese
- ¼ cup diced sun-dried tomatoes
- ¼ cup diced onion
- 1 teaspoon dried oregano
- ½ teaspoon garlic powder
- Salt and pepper to taste
- Cooking spray

Instructions

1. Preheat oven to 375°F. Spray 8x8" baking dish with cooking spray.
2. Whisk eggs, milk, oregano, garlic powder, salt, and pepper.
3. Stir in spinach, feta, tomatoes, and onion.
4. Pour into prepared dish.
5. Bake 25–28 minutes until center is set and edges are lightly golden.
6. Cool 5 minutes, cut into 4 squares.

Nutrition (per square)

- Calories: 195
- Protein: 22g
- Carbohydrates: 6g
- Fat: 12g
- Fiber: 1g
- Sugar: 4g

Substitutions

- Use egg whites (12 total) for lower fat
- Replace feta with goat cheese or shredded mozzarella
- Add mushrooms or bell peppers

Storage

Refrigerate up to 5 days. Reheat individual squares in microwave 60 seconds.

Tip: Line baking dish with parchment for easier removal and serving.

Peanut Butter Protein Smoothie Bowl

◔ Quick | ◯ High Protein | 🥣 Gentle | 🌿 Plant-Based

Why it works: Smoothie bowls provide the same nutrition as drinkable smoothies but with a thicker texture that feels more substantial. The combination of protein powder, peanut butter, and Greek yogurt delivers muscle-supporting protein, while the toppings add texture and nutrients. This format may be easier to consume slowly when appetite is reduced.

Prep time: 6 minutes

Cook time: 0 minutes

Protein: 38g

Ingredients

- 1 scoop chocolate protein powder (25g protein)
- ½ cup plain non-fat Greek yogurt
- ½ cup unsweetened almond milk
- 1 tablespoon peanut butter
- ½ frozen banana
- 1 tablespoon cocoa powder
- ½ cup ice
- Toppings: 1 tablespoon granola, 1 teaspoon chia seeds, sliced banana

Instructions

1. Combine protein powder, Greek yogurt, almond milk, peanut butter, frozen banana, cocoa powder, and ice in blender.
2. Blend until thick and creamy, about 60 seconds.
3. Pour into bowl.
4. Arrange toppings on surface.
5. Eat with spoon.

Nutrition (per serving)

- Calories: 410
- Protein: 38g
- Carbohydrates: 38g
- Fat: 13g
- Fiber: 7g
- Sugar: 18g

Substitutions

- Use vanilla protein powder and omit cocoa
- Replace peanut butter with almond butter
- Use regular milk for higher protein

Storage

Not suitable for storage. Consume immediately after preparation.

Tip: Use less liquid than regular smoothies for proper bowl consistency.

Ham and Cheese Egg Cups

⏱ Quick | 🥚 High Protein | 👨‍👩‍👧 Family Friendly

Why it works: Ham serves as both a protein source and an edible "cup" that eliminates the need for bread or pastry. This creative format reduces carbohydrates while delivering concentrated protein. The individual portions are perfect for portion control and can be eaten with one hand, ideal for busy mornings.

Prep time: 5 minutes

Cook time: 15 minutes

Protein: 18g (per 2 cups)

Ingredients (makes 6 cups)

- 6 slices deli ham (low-sodium)
- 6 large eggs
- ¼ cup shredded reduced-fat cheese
- 2 tablespoons diced bell pepper
- 1 tablespoon chopped chives
- Black pepper to taste
- Cooking spray

Instructions

1. Preheat oven to 375°F. Spray muffin tin with cooking spray.
2. Press one ham slice into each muffin cup, forming a cup shape.
3. Divide cheese and bell pepper among ham cups.
4. Crack one egg into each cup.
5. Sprinkle with chives and black pepper.
6. Bake 15–17 minutes until egg whites are set but yolks are still slightly soft.
7. Cool 3 minutes before removing.

Nutrition (per 2 cups)

- Calories: 220
- Protein: 18g
- Carbohydrates: 2g
- Fat: 14g
- Fiber: 0g
- Sugar: 1g

Substitutions

- Use turkey slices instead of ham
- Replace cheese with crumbled feta
- Add spinach or tomatoes

Storage

Refrigerate up to 4 days. Reheat in microwave 30–45 seconds.

Tip: Use thicker deli ham slices to prevent tearing when forming cups.

Protein Banana Bread Muffins

◯ High Protein | 👨‍👩‍👧 Family Friendly

Why it works: These muffins transform traditional banana bread into a high-protein breakfast option by incorporating protein powder and Greek yogurt. Each muffin provides substantial protein in a portable, familiar format. The natural sweetness from banana reduces the need for added sugar while keeping the recipe gentle on sensitive stomachs.

Prep time: 10 minutes

Cook time: 18 minutes

Protein: 10g (per muffin, makes 12)

Ingredients

- 2 ripe bananas, mashed
- ½ cup plain non-fat Greek yogurt
- 2 large eggs
- 1 scoop vanilla protein powder (20g protein)
- 1 cup oat flour
- ¼ cup honey
- 1 teaspoon baking powder
- ½ teaspoon baking soda
- 1 teaspoon vanilla extract
- ½ teaspoon cinnamon

- Pinch of salt
- Cooking spray

Instructions

1. Preheat oven to 350°F. Spray muffin tin with cooking spray.
2. Mix mashed bananas, Greek yogurt, eggs, honey, and vanilla.
3. In separate bowl, combine protein powder, oat flour, baking powder, baking soda, cinnamon, and salt.
4. Fold dry ingredients into wet ingredients until just combined.
5. Divide batter among 12 muffin cups.
6. Bake 18–20 minutes until toothpick comes out clean.
7. Cool 10 minutes before removing from tin.

Nutrition (per muffin)

- Calories: 110
- Protein: 10g
- Carbohydrates: 16g
- Fat: 2g
- Fiber: 2g
- Sugar: 7g

Substitutions

- Use almond flour instead of oat flour
- Replace honey with maple syrup
- Add ¼ cup chocolate chips or walnuts

Storage

Refrigerate up to 5 days or freeze up to 3 months. Thaw overnight or microwave 30 seconds.

Tip: Eat 2 muffins for a complete 20g protein breakfast.

Savory Cottage Cheese Toast

⏱ Quick | ◯ High Protein | 🥣 Gentle

Why it works: Cottage cheese provides concentrated protein with a mild flavor that's well-tolerated by most GLP-1 users. Spreading it on high-protein bread creates a satisfying breakfast that's easy to prepare and eat. The savory toppings add flavor and nutrients without overwhelming reduced appetite.

Prep time: 5 minutes

Cook time: 2 minutes

Protein: 28g

Ingredients

- 2 slices high-protein bread (6g+ protein per slice)
- ½ cup low-fat cottage cheese
- 1 medium tomato, sliced
- ¼ avocado, sliced
- 1 tablespoon everything bagel seasoning
- Red pepper flakes (optional)
- Black pepper to taste

Instructions

1. Toast bread until golden.
2. Spread cottage cheese evenly on both slices.
3. Top with tomato and avocado slices.
4. Sprinkle with everything bagel seasoning and black pepper.
5. Add red pepper flakes if desired.

Nutrition (per serving)

- Calories: 320
- Protein: 28g
- Carbohydrates: 32g
- Fat: 10g
- Fiber: 10g
- Sugar: 6g

Substitutions

- Use rice cakes for gluten-free option
- Replace cottage cheese with ricotta
- Add smoked salmon for extra protein

Storage

Best eaten fresh. Cottage cheese can be prepared 1 day ahead; assemble just before eating.

Tip: Whip cottage cheese in blender for smoother, cream cheese-like texture.

Protein-Packed Breakfast Quinoa

🕐 Quick | 🥚 High Protein | 🥣 Gentle | 🌿 Plant-Based

Why it works: Quinoa is a complete protein containing all essential amino acids, making it ideal for muscle preservation. Cooking it with protein powder and milk boosts the protein content to therapeutic levels. This warm, porridge-like breakfast is gentle on the stomach and provides sustained energy without blood sugar spikes.

Prep time: 3 minutes

Cook time: 15 minutes

Protein: 26g

Ingredients

- ½ cup quinoa, rinsed
- 1 cup unsweetened almond milk
- ½ cup water
- 1 scoop vanilla protein powder (20g protein)
- 1 tablespoon almond butter
- ½ teaspoon cinnamon
- Pinch of salt
- Toppings: ¼ cup berries, 1 tablespoon sliced almonds

Instructions

1. Combine quinoa, almond milk, water, cinnamon, and salt in saucepan.
2. Bring to boil, reduce heat to low, cover.
3. Simmer 15 minutes until liquid is absorbed.
4. Remove from heat, stir in protein powder until smooth.
5. Top with almond butter, berries, and almonds.

Nutrition (per serving)

- Calories: 380
- Protein: 26g
- Carbohydrates: 42g
- Fat: 12g
- Fiber: 7g
- Sugar: 4g

Substitutions

- Use regular milk for higher protein
- Replace quinoa with steel-cut oats
- Try chocolate protein powder with cocoa nibs

Storage

Refrigerate up to 4 days. Add splash of milk when reheating; microwave 90 seconds.

Tip: Cook quinoa in batches; reheat portions with protein powder added fresh.

Mediterranean Egg Scramble

⏱ Quick | ◯ High Protein | 👨‍👩‍👧 Family Friendly

Why it works: This scramble incorporates Mediterranean flavors and ingredients known for their health benefits. The combination of eggs, feta, and olives provides protein and healthy fats that support satiety. The vegetables add fiber and micronutrients while keeping the dish light and digestible.

Prep time: 5 minutes

Cook time: 7 minutes

Protein: 24g

Ingredients

- 3 large eggs
- ¼ cup crumbled feta cheese
- ½ cup cherry tomatoes, halved
- ¼ cup diced cucumber
- 2 tablespoons sliced Kalamata olives
- 1 cup fresh spinach
- 1 teaspoon olive oil
- ½ teaspoon dried oregano
- Black pepper to taste

Instructions

1. Heat olive oil in skillet over medium heat.
2. Add cherry tomatoes, cook 2 minutes.
3. Add spinach, cook until wilted, about 1 minute.
4. Whisk eggs with oregano and pepper, pour into skillet.
5. Scramble eggs, stirring gently, about 3 minutes.
6. Remove from heat, stir in feta and olives.
7. Top with fresh cucumber.

Nutrition (per serving)

- Calories: 310
- Protein: 24g
- Carbohydrates: 8g
- Fat: 21g
- Fiber: 2g
- Sugar: 4g

Substitutions

- Use goat cheese instead of feta
- Replace olives with sun-dried tomatoes
- Add artichoke hearts

Storage

Refrigerate up to 3 days. Reheat gently in microwave 45 seconds. Add fresh cucumber after reheating.

Tip: Add cucumber after cooking to maintain crisp texture.

Protein Coffee Shake

Why it works: This shake combines coffee with protein for a breakfast that addresses both energy and nutrition needs. The caffeine can help with morning fatigue common in early GLP-1 use, while the protein supports muscle preservation. The cold, smooth texture is often well-tolerated when solid food feels unappealing.

Prep time: 4 minutes

Cook time: 0 minutes

Protein: 32g

Ingredients

- 1 cup cold brew coffee (or chilled regular coffee)
- 1 scoop chocolate protein powder (25g protein)
- ½ cup unsweetened almond milk
- 2 tablespoons plain non-fat Greek yogurt
- 1 teaspoon cocoa powder
- ½ cup ice
- Optional: 5 drops liquid stevia

Instructions

1. Add coffee, protein powder, almond milk, Greek yogurt, and cocoa powder to blender.
2. Add ice and sweetener if using.
3. Blend on high 45 seconds until smooth and frothy.
4. Pour into glass.

Nutrition (per serving)

- Calories: 200
- Protein: 32g
- Carbohydrates: 10g
- Fat: 4g
- Fiber: 3g
- Sugar: 3g

Substitutions

- Use vanilla protein powder for mocha flavor
- Replace coffee with chai tea
- Add 1 tablespoon peanut butter for extra calories

Storage

Best consumed immediately. Can refrigerate up to 4 hours; shake well before drinking.

Tip: Brew coffee the night before and refrigerate for quick morning preparation.

Key Takeaways

- **Prioritize protein at breakfast** to support muscle preservation and enhance satiety throughout the day. Target 25–30g per meal.
- **Choose easily digestible protein sources** like eggs, Greek yogurt, and cottage cheese, which are well-tolerated by most GLP-1 users.
- **Prepare meals in advance** when possible. Many recipes can be made in batches and stored for 3–5 days, reducing morning effort.
- **Start with smaller portions** if appetite is low. You can always eat more, but forcing large portions may increase nausea.
- **Combine protein with moderate healthy fats** from sources like nuts, avocado, and olive oil to support sustained energy and vitamin absorption.
- **Keep backup options ready**. Smoothies and protein shakes are ideal for mornings when solid food feels overwhelming.

- **Don't skip breakfast** even if appetite is low. Consistent meal timing helps prevent energy crashes and makes it easier to meet daily protein targets.

- **Experiment with textures**. Some users tolerate creamy foods (yogurt, smoothies) better than solid foods, especially in early treatment phases.

Chapter 10:
Quick & Balanced Lunches

Lunch on GLP-1 medication requires a thoughtful approach. With a reduced appetite, you might skip this meal or struggle to finish it. However, skipping lunch can lead to energy dips, muscle loss, and overeating later.

The solution is small, protein-centered plates that are not overwhelming. These 20 recipes are tailored to accommodate your body's delayed gastric emptying. Each one offers 20–35 grams of protein in manageable portions, even when your appetite is low.

The options include chicken, seafood, and plant-based proteins, many ready in under 20 minutes. They are structured to preserve lean muscle while supporting steady weight loss.

These meals are not heavy. They are strategic plates designed to supply your body with high-quality protein, gentle textures, and balanced nutrition that won't cause discomfort.

Mediterranean Chicken Bowl

Quick | High Protein | Plant-Based Options

Prep time: 10 minutes

Cook time: 12 minutes

Servings: 1

Why It Works

Grilled chicken provides lean, easily digestible protein. Quinoa offers complex carbs without heaviness, while cucumbers and tomatoes add volume and hydration without straining digestion.

Ingredients

- 4 oz boneless, skinless chicken breast
- ½ cup cooked quinoa
- ½ cup cherry tomatoes, halved
- ½ cup cucumber, diced
- 2 tbsp crumbled feta cheese
- 1 tbsp olive oil
- 1 tbsp lemon juice
- ½ tsp dried oregano
- Salt and pepper to taste
- 2 cups mixed greens

Instructions

1. Season chicken with oregano, salt, and pepper. Grill or pan-sear over medium-high heat for 5–6 minutes per side until fully cooked.
2. Let chicken rest for 3 minutes, then slice.
3. Arrange greens in a bowl. Top with quinoa, tomatoes, cucumber, and chicken.
4. Drizzle with olive oil and lemon juice. Sprinkle with feta.

Nutrition (per serving)

- Calories: 385
- Protein: 38g
- Carbohydrates: 28g
- Fat: 14g
- Fiber: 5g

Substitutions

- Plant-based: Use firm tofu or chickpeas instead of chicken
- Grain-free: Swap quinoa for cauliflower rice
- Dairy-free: Omit feta or use a dairy-free alternative

Storage Tips

Store components separately for up to 3 days. Keep dressing separate until serving. Chicken stays fresh for 3 days in the refrigerator.

Tip: Prep quinoa and chicken in batches for easy assembly throughout the week.

Ginger-Lime Shrimp Lettuce Wraps

Prep time: 8 minutes

Cook time: 5 minutes

Servings: 1

Why It Works

Shrimp cooks quickly and provides high-quality protein that's easy to digest. Ginger helps soothe nausea, a common GLP-1 side effect. Lettuce wraps keep the meal light.

Ingredients

- 5 oz medium shrimp, peeled and deveined
- 1 tsp fresh ginger, grated
- 1 tsp lime juice
- 1 tsp olive oil
- 4 large butter lettuce leaves
- ¼ cup shredded carrots
- ¼ cup thinly sliced bell pepper
- 1 tbsp chopped cilantro
- 1 tsp low-sodium soy sauce

Instructions

1. Heat olive oil in a skillet over medium-high heat.
2. Add shrimp and ginger. Cook for 2–3 minutes until shrimp turn pink.
3. Remove from heat and toss with lime juice and soy sauce.
4. Arrange lettuce leaves on a plate. Divide shrimp, carrots, and bell pepper among leaves.
5. Garnish with cilantro.

Nutrition (per serving)

- Calories: 215
- Protein: 32g
- Carbohydrates: 9g
- Fat: 6g
- Fiber: 3g

Substitutions

- Shellfish-free: Use diced chicken breast
- Low-FODMAP: Omit garlic if added; use green onion tops only
- Spice-free: Reduce or omit ginger

Storage Tips

Best eaten fresh. Cooked shrimp can be refrigerated for 1 day. Store lettuce separately.

Tip: Double the shrimp batch and use extras in a salad the next day.

White Bean & Spinach Soup

🌿 Plant-Based | 🥣 Gentle | ◯ High Protein

Prep time: 5 minutes

Cook time: 15 minutes

Servings: 2

Why It Works

Soup is ideal when solid foods feel heavy. White beans deliver plant-based protein and fiber. The smooth texture is gentle on the stomach, and the warm liquid aids digestion.

Ingredients

- 1 can (15 oz) white beans, drained and rinsed
- 2 cups low-sodium vegetable broth
- 2 cups fresh spinach
- 1 clove garlic, minced
- ½ tsp olive oil
- ¼ tsp dried thyme
- Pinch red pepper flakes (optional)
- Salt and pepper to taste

Instructions

1. Heat olive oil in a pot over medium heat. Add garlic and cook briefly.
2. Add broth, beans, and thyme. Simmer for 10 minutes.
3. Use an immersion blender to partially blend (leave some beans whole).
4. Stir in spinach and cook until wilted.
5. Season with salt, pepper, and red pepper flakes if desired.

Nutrition (per serving)

- Calories: 195
- Protein: 12g
- Carbohydrates: 32g
- Fat: 2g
- Fiber: 9g

Substitutions

- Higher protein: Add diced cooked chicken
- Creamier texture: Stir in Greek yogurt
- Different greens: Use kale

Storage Tips

Refrigerate up to 4 days. Freezes well for up to 2 months.

Tip: Make a double batch and freeze portions for easy meals.

Turkey & Avocado Collard Wrap

Prep time: 7 minutes

Cook time: 0 minutes

Servings: 1

Why It Works

No cooking required, perfect for low-energy days. Turkey provides lean protein, while avocado adds healthy fats that support nutrient absorption. Collard greens replace tortillas.

Ingredients

- 2 large collard green leaves, stems trimmed
- 3 oz sliced turkey breast
- ¼ avocado, sliced
- 2 tbsp hummus
- ¼ cup shredded carrots
- 2 tbsp diced cucumber
- Pinch of black pepper

Instructions

1. Blanch collard leaves briefly to soften. Pat dry.
2. Lay leaves flat, overlapping.
3. Spread hummus down the center.
4. Layer turkey, avocado, carrots, and cucumber.
5. Fold sides in and roll tightly. Slice in half.

Nutrition (per serving)

- Calories: 285
- Protein: 28g
- Carbohydrates: 18g
- Fat: 11g
- Fiber: 8g

Substitutions

- Plant-based: Use tempeh or chickpea salad
- Nut-free: Use mashed white beans instead of hummus
- Different wrap: Use romaine leaves

Storage Tips

Assemble just before eating to prevent sogginess. Prep components separately for 2 days.

Tip: Pack components separately for a workspace-friendly lunch.

Baked Cod with Lemon & Herbs

🕙 Quick | 🥚 High Protein | 🥣 Gentle | 👨‍👩‍👧 Family Friendly

Prep time: 5 minutes

Cook time: 12 minutes

Servings: 1

Why It Works

Cod is mild, lean, and easy to digest. Baking requires minimal effort, and the light lemon flavor won't cause nausea.

Ingredients

- 5 oz cod fillet
- 1 tsp olive oil
- 1 tsp lemon juice
- ½ tsp dried dill
- ¼ tsp garlic powder
- Salt and pepper to taste
- Lemon wedge for serving

Side suggestion: 1 cup steamed green beans

Instructions

1. Preheat oven to 400°F. Line a baking sheet with parchment.
2. Place cod on sheet. Brush with olive oil and lemon juice.
3. Sprinkle with dill, garlic powder, salt, and pepper.
4. Bake for 10–12 minutes until fish flakes easily.
5. Serve with lemon wedge and green beans.

Nutrition (per serving, fish only)

- Calories: 155
- Protein: 28g
- Carbohydrates: 1g
- Fat: 5g
- Fiber: 0g

Substitutions

- Different fish: Use tilapia or haddock
- Herb variations: Try parsley or thyme
- Higher calories: Add roasted sweet potato

Storage Tips

Best eaten fresh. Refrigerate for up to 2 days.

Tip: Cod cooks quickly—check at 10 minutes to avoid overcooking.

Chickpea Salad Plate

Prep time: 10 minutes

Cook time: 0 minutes

Servings: 1

Why It Works

Chickpeas provide plant-based protein and fiber-rich fullness without heaviness. Fresh vegetables add volume and nutrition with minimal calories.

Ingredients

- 1 cup canned chickpeas, drained and rinsed
- 1 tbsp tahini
- 1 tsp lemon juice
- ¼ tsp cumin
- 1 cup mixed greens
- ¼ cup cherry tomatoes, halved
- ¼ cup diced cucumber
- 2 tbsp diced red onion
- Salt and pepper to taste

Instructions

1. Mash half the chickpeas with a fork in a bowl.
2. Add tahini, lemon juice, cumin, salt, and pepper. Mix well.
3. Stir in remaining chickpeas.
4. Serve over mixed greens with tomatoes, cucumber, and red onion.

Nutrition (per serving)

- Calories: 310
- Protein: 14g
- Carbohydrates: 42g
- Fat: 9g
- Fiber: 12g

Substitutions

- Higher protein: Add grilled chicken
- Nut-free: Use mashed avocado instead of tahini
- Grain addition: Serve with farro

Storage Tips

Chickpea mixture keeps for 3 days. Store greens separately.

Tip: Prep chickpea mixture in advance for quick assembly during the week.

Egg Salad Lettuce Cups

⏱ Quick | ◯ High Protein | 🥣 Gentle

Prep time: 10 minutes

Cook time: 10 minutes (for eggs)

Servings: 1

Why It Works

Eggs offer complete protein that's easy to digest. Lettuce cups keep the meal light, and the creamy texture is gentle on a sensitive stomach.

Ingredients

- 2 large hard-boiled eggs, chopped
- 1 tbsp plain Greek yogurt
- 1 tsp Dijon mustard
- 1 tbsp diced celery
- 1 tbsp diced red bell pepper
- Pinch paprika
- Salt and pepper to taste
- 4 large butter lettuce leaves

Instructions

1. Combine eggs, Greek yogurt, and mustard in a bowl.
2. Stir in celery and bell pepper. Season with paprika, salt, and pepper.
3. Spoon mixture into lettuce leaves.

Nutrition (per serving)

- Calories: 195
- Protein: 16g
- Carbohydrates: 6g
- Fat: 12g
- Fiber: 2g

Substitutions

- Dairy-free: Use mashed avocado instead of yogurt
- Lower fat: Use egg whites only
- Bread option: Serve on whole-grain toast if preferred

Storage Tips

Egg salad keeps for 2 days. Store separately from lettuce.

Tip: Make egg salad the night before for an easy lunch.

Grilled Salmon with Cucumber Salad

⏱ Quick | ◯ High Protein | 👨‍👧 Family Friendly

Prep time: 8 minutes

Cook time: 8 minutes

Servings: 1

Why It Works

Salmon provides high-quality protein and omega-3s that support metabolic health. The cool cucumber salad is refreshing and won't overwhelm your appetite.

Ingredients

- 4 oz salmon fillet
- ½ tsp olive oil
- ¼ tsp dried dill
- Salt and pepper to taste

Cucumber Salad:

- 1 cup sliced cucumber
- 2 tbsp plain Greek yogurt
- 1 tsp lemon juice
- 1 tsp fresh dill (or ½ tsp dried)
- Pinch salt

Instructions

1. Preheat grill to medium-high.
2. Brush salmon with olive oil. Season with dill, salt, and pepper.
3. Grill for 4 minutes per side until salmon flakes.
4. Combine cucumber, yogurt, lemon juice, dill, and salt.
5. Serve salmon with cucumber salad.

Nutrition (per serving)

- Calories: 265
- Protein: 30g
- Carbohydrates: 6g
- Fat: 13g
- Fiber: 1g

Substitutions

- Different fish: Use trout or arctic char
- Dairy-free: Use tahini-lemon dressing instead of yogurt
- Extra vegetables: Add cherry tomatoes

Storage Tips

Salmon is best fresh. Cucumber salad keeps for 2 days.

Tip: Leftover salmon works well in a salad the next day.

Lentil & Vegetable Stew

🌿 Plant-Based | 🍲 Gentle | 👨‍👩‍👧 Family Friendly

Prep time: 10 minutes

Cook time: 25 minutes

Servings: 3

Why It Works

Lentils provide protein and fiber. The stew is easy to eat in small portions, and the warm, soft texture is gentle on digestion.

Ingredients

- 1 cup dried green or brown lentils, rinsed
- 3 cups low-sodium vegetable broth
- 1 cup diced carrots
- 1 cup diced zucchini
- ½ cup diced tomatoes
- 1 clove garlic, minced
- ½ tsp cumin
- ½ tsp smoked paprika
- Salt and pepper to taste

Instructions

1. Combine lentils, broth, carrots, garlic, cumin, and paprika in a pot.
2. Bring to a boil, then reduce heat and simmer for 20 minutes.
3. Add zucchini and tomatoes. Cook 5 more minutes until lentils are tender.
4. Season with salt and pepper.

Nutrition (per serving)

- Calories: 220
- Protein: 14g
- Carbohydrates: 38g
- Fat: 1g
- Fiber: 10g

Substitutions

- Higher protein: Add cooked chicken
- Different vegetables: Use spinach or bell peppers
- Creamier texture: Add Greek yogurt

Storage Tips

Refrigerate up to 5 days. Freezes well for 3 months.

Tip: Great for meal prep—portion into containers for lunches.

Tuna Cucumber Boats

⏱ Quick | ◯ High Protein | 🥣 Gentle

Prep time: 8 minutes

Cook time: 0 minutes

Servings: 1

Why It Works

No cooking, minimal prep, and high protein make this ideal for days with low appetite. Cucumber adds hydration and crunch without heaviness.

Ingredients

- 1 can (5 oz) tuna in water, drained
- 1 tbsp plain Greek yogurt
- 1 tsp Dijon mustard
- 1 tbsp diced celery
- 1 tbsp diced red onion
- Salt and pepper to taste
- 1 large cucumber, halved lengthwise and seeded

Instructions

1. Mix tuna, Greek yogurt, mustard, celery, and onion in a bowl. Season with salt and pepper.
2. Scoop seeds from cucumber halves to create "boats."
3. Fill each cucumber boat with tuna mixture.

Nutrition (per serving)

- Calories: 210
- Protein: 35g
- Carbohydrates: 8g
- Fat: 4g
- Fiber: 2g

Substitutions

- Different protein: Use canned salmon or shredded chicken
- Dairy-free: Use mashed avocado instead of yogurt
- Bread option: Serve on whole-grain crackers

Storage Tips

Tuna mixture keeps for 2 days. Assemble cucumber boats just before eating.

Tip: Pack tuna mixture and cucumber separately for lunch on the go.

Common Mistakes to Avoid

- Skipping lunch entirely: Even with a reduced appetite, consistent protein intake protects muscle mass.
- Choosing only cold foods: Warm soups and cooked proteins may be easier to tolerate.
- Ignoring prep work: Batch-cooking proteins and grains simplifies weekday meals.
- Overloading portions: Start with smaller servings; you can always have more later.
- Forgetting hydration: Drink water throughout your meal to assist digestion.
- Relying on processed foods: Whole foods offer better nutrient density for reduced calorie intake.

- Protein at every lunch preserves muscle mass during GLP-1-assisted weight loss.

- Small, balanced plates prevent nausea while delivering essential nutrients.

- Prep-friendly recipes reduce decision fatigue on low-energy days.

- Gentle cooking methods like baking and grilling are easier on slowed digestion.

- Mix protein sources throughout the week—chicken, seafood, eggs, and plant-based options.

- Soups and wraps offer flexibility when solid meals feel too heavy.

- Batch cooking proteins and grains makes weekday assembly stress-free.

- Listen to your body's signals - eat slowly and stop when comfortably satisfied, not full.

Chapter 11:
Muscle-Protecting Dinners

GLP-1 medications can aid in weight loss, but without the right nutrition strategy, you risk losing muscle. This chapter presents 20 high-protein dinner recipes aimed at preserving lean mass while accommodating a reduced appetite.

Each recipe offers at least 30 grams of protein per serving - the amount research suggests is optimal for muscle protein synthesis. These meals ensure satisfaction in smaller portions and are gentle on the stomach. Options include poultry, beef, fish, and plant-based proteins to maintain variety and sustainability.

Muscle preservation involves not just protein quantity but timing. Dinners should align with your natural eating window and be ideally paired with resistance training earlier in the day. While a post-workout meal within 30–60 minutes is beneficial, consistent daily protein intake holds more significance than timing alone.

The recipes are categorized by protein type and detail prep times, nutritional information, storage guidelines, and substitutions. Icons indicate characteristics such as quick prep, family-friendly, gentle on the stomach, or plant-based.

The aim is consistency, not perfection. Use these recipes to build sustainable eating habits that protect muscle while losing fat.

Lemon Herb Chicken Thighs with Roasted Vegetables

◯ High Protein | 👨‍👩‍👧 Family Friendly

Why It Works:

Chicken thighs deliver 35g of protein per serving and remain moist and flavorful, key when appetite is low. Their higher fat content compared to chicken breasts ensures satisfaction in smaller portions. Roasted vegetables contribute fiber and micronutrients without overwhelming the stomach.

Prep Time: 10 minutes

Cook Time: 35 minutes

Servings: 4

Ingredients:

- 1.5 lbs boneless, skinless chicken thighs
- 2 tbsp olive oil
- 2 lemons (zested and juiced)
- 3 garlic cloves, minced
- 1 tsp dried oregano
- 1 tsp dried thyme
- 1/2 tsp sea salt
- 1/4 tsp black pepper

- 2 cups broccoli florets
- 1 red bell pepper, chopped
- 1 zucchini, sliced

Instructions:

1. Preheat oven to 425°F.
2. Combine olive oil, lemon zest, juice, garlic, herbs, salt, and pepper.
3. Coat chicken with half the marinade in a baking dish.
4. Toss vegetables with remaining marinade, arranging around chicken.
5. Roast for 30–35 minutes until chicken reaches 165°F.
6. Rest 5 minutes before serving.

Nutrition (per serving):

Calories: 320 | Protein: 35g | Carbs: 12g | Fat: 15g | Fiber: 4g

Substitutions:

Chicken breast (reduce cook time) | Turkey thighs | Swap vegetables as desired

Storage:

Refrigerate up to 4 days. Reheat gently.

Tip: Marinate chicken 2–4 hours in advance for enhanced flavor.

Turkey Meatballs in Tomato Basil Sauce

◯ High Protein | 👨‍👩 Family Friendly | 🍲 Gentle

Why It Works:

Ground turkey stays moist as meatballs. The tomato sauce offers a gentle acidity well-tolerated by many GLP-1 users. With 38g of protein per serving, it supports muscle synthesis in small portions.

Prep Time: 15 minutes

Cook Time: 25 minutes

Servings: 4

- Ingredients:
- 1.5 lbs ground turkey (93% lean)
- 1/2 cup almond flour
- 1 egg
- 2 garlic cloves, minced
- 1 tsp Italian seasoning
- 1/2 tsp sea salt
- 1/4 tsp black pepper
- 1 tbsp olive oil
- 2 cups crushed tomatoes
- 1/4 cup fresh basil, chopped
- 1/4 tsp red pepper flakes (optional)

Instructions:

1. Mix turkey, almond flour, egg, garlic, seasoning, salt, and pepper.
2. Form into 16 meatballs.
3. Brown meatballs in olive oil over medium heat.
4. Add crushed tomatoes, basil, and red pepper flakes; simmer covered until cooked through.

Nutrition (per serving):

Calories: 310 | Protein: 38g | Carbs: 10g | Fat: 13g | Fiber: 3g

Substitutions:

Ground chicken | Lean ground beef | Marinara sauce substitution

Storage:

Refrigerate up to 4 days or freeze up to 3 months.

Tip: Serve over zucchini noodles or cauliflower rice for added volume.

Greek Chicken Bowls with Tzatziki

◯ High Protein | 👨‍👩‍👧 Family Friendly

Why It Works:

The bowl offers 36g protein with bright flavors, combating taste changes some GLP-1 users experience. Tzatziki adds creaminess and probiotics, supporting digestion. Cucumber and tomato provide hydration and fiber.

Prep Time: 15 minutes

Cook Time: 20 minutes

Servings: 4

Ingredients:

For chicken:

- 1.5 lbs chicken breast, cubed
- 2 tbsp olive oil
- 1 tbsp lemon juice
- 2 tsp dried oregano
- 1 tsp garlic powder
- 1/2 tsp sea salt
- 1/4 tsp black pepper

For bowls:

- 2 cups cooked quinoa
- 1 cucumber, diced
- 1 cup cherry tomatoes, halved
- 1/4 red onion, thinly sliced
- 1/2 cup kalamata olives

For tzatziki:

- 1 cup plain Greek yogurt
- 1/2 cucumber, grated and drained
- 1 garlic clove, minced
- 1 tbsp lemon juice
- 1 tbsp fresh dill

Instructions:

1. Toss chicken with olive oil, lemon juice, and spices.
2. Cook in a skillet until golden and cooked through.
3. Mix tzatziki ingredients.
4. Assemble bowls with quinoa, chicken, vegetables, olives, and tzatziki.

Nutrition (per serving):

Calories: 385 | Protein: 36g | Carbs: 32g | Fat: 12g | Fiber: 5g

Substitutions:

Cauliflower rice | Turkey breast | Shrimp

Storage:

Store components separately. Chicken and tzatziki last 3 days; quinoa lasts 5 days.

Tip: Prep chicken and tzatziki ahead for quick assembly.

Korean Beef Lettuce Cups

⏱ Quick | ◯ High Protein | 👫 Family Friendly

Why It Works:

Ground beef provides bioavailable protein and iron. The Korean-inspired sauce is appealing, even with reduced appetite. Offering 32g of protein per serving, it supports muscle synthesis in small portions.

Prep Time: 8 minutes

Cook Time: 10 minutes

Servings: 4

Ingredients:

- 1.5 lbs lean ground beef
- 2 tbsp coconut aminos
- 1 tbsp sesame oil
- 2 garlic cloves, minced
- 1 tsp fresh ginger, grated
- 1 tbsp rice vinegar
- 1/2 tsp red pepper flakes
- 2 green onions, sliced
- 1 tbsp sesame seeds

- 12 butter lettuce leaves
- 1 cup shredded carrots

Instructions:

1. Brown beef; drain fat.
2. Add coconut aminos, sesame oil, garlic, ginger, and vinegar; cook until sauce thickens.
3. Stir in green onions and sesame seeds.
4. Serve in lettuce cups topped with carrots.

Nutrition (per serving):

Calories: 295 | Protein: 32g | Carbs: 6g | Fat: 15g | Fiber: 2g

Substitutions:

Ground turkey | Chicken | Tempeh

Storage:

Refrigerate filling up to 4 days. Store lettuce separately.

Tip: Double the recipe for leftovers over cauliflower rice.

Beef and Broccoli Stir-Fry

◯ High Protein | 👨‍👩‍👧 Family Friendly

Why It Works:

Flank steak delivers 35g protein per serving. Broccoli provides fiber and vitamin C, enhancing immune function. Quick cooking retains nutrients and tenderness.

Prep Time: 12 minutes (plus 15 minutes marinating)

Cook Time: 10 minutes

Servings: 4

Ingredients:

- 1.5 lbs flank steak, sliced thin
- 4 cups broccoli florets
- 2 tbsp avocado oil
- 3 garlic cloves, minced
- 1 tbsp fresh ginger, grated

For marinade:

- 3 tbsp coconut aminos
- 1 tbsp rice vinegar
- 1 tsp sesame oil
- 1/2 tsp black pepper

Instructions:

1. Marinate beef for 15 minutes.
2. Sear beef in oil. Remove and set aside.
3. Stir-fry broccoli, garlic, and ginger.
4. Return beef to combine.

Nutrition (per serving):

Calories: 310 | Protein: 35g | Carbs: 10g | Fat: 14g | Fiber: 3g

Substitutions:

Sirloin steak | Chicken breast | Snap peas

Storage:

Refrigerate up to 3 days.

Tip: Freeze beef briefly before slicing for thinner cuts.

Lemon Garlic Salmon with Asparagus

⏱ Quick | ⬭ High Protein | 🍲 Gentle

Why It Works:

Salmon provides 34g of protein and omega-3 fatty acids supporting muscle recovery and inflammation reduction. The quick cooking preserves nutrients.

Prep Time: 8 minutes

Cook Time: 15 minutes

Servings: 4

Ingredients:

- 4 salmon fillets (6 oz each)
- 1 lb asparagus
- 3 tbsp olive oil
- 3 garlic cloves, minced
- 2 lemons
- 1/2 tsp sea salt
- 1/4 tsp black pepper
- 2 tbsp fresh parsley

Instructions:

1. Preheat oven to 400°F.
2. Arrange salmon and asparagus on a baking sheet.
3. Mix olive oil, garlic, lemon zest, juice, salt, and pepper; brush over fish and asparagus.
4. Bake until salmon flakes easily.

Nutrition (per serving):

Calories: 340 | Protein: 34g | Carbs: 6g | Fat: 20g | Fiber: 3g

Substitutions:

Arctic char | Trout | Green beans

Storage:

Refrigerate up to 2 days.

Tip: Check salmon at 12 minutes to prevent drying.

Blackened Cod with Mango Salsa

◌ High Protein | 🥣 Gentle

Why It Works:

Cod is mild, lean, and easy to digest. The mango salsa adds vitamin C, with 32g protein ensuring muscle maintenance without heaviness.

Prep Time: 12 minutes

Cook Time: 10 minutes

Servings: 4

Ingredients:

For cod:

- 4 cod fillets (6 oz each)
- 1 tbsp olive oil
- 1 tsp paprika
- 1 tsp garlic powder
- 1/2 tsp onion powder
- 1/2 tsp cumin
- 1/4 tsp cayenne pepper
- 1/2 tsp sea salt

For salsa:

- 1 mango, diced
- 1/2 red bell pepper, diced
- 1/4 red onion, diced
- 1 jalapeño, minced
- 2 tbsp fresh cilantro
- 1 lime, juiced

Instructions:

1. Mix spices; rub over cod.
2. Cook cod in olive oil until flaky.
3. Combine salsa ingredients.
4. Serve cod with salsa.

Nutrition (per serving):

Calories: 220 | Protein: 32g | Carbs: 14g | Fat: 4g | Fiber: 2g

Substitutions:

Halibut | Mahi-mahi | Pineapple salsa

Storage:

Refrigerate separately up to 2 days.

Tip: Adjust cayenne if sensitive to spice.

Tempeh Stir-Fry with Peanut Sauce

◯ High Protein | 🌿 Plant-Based

Why It Works:

Tempeh offers 31g of protein and is easier to digest. The peanut sauce provides healthy fats and flavor, satisfying even in smaller portions.

Prep Time: 12 minutes

Cook Time: 12 minutes

Servings: 4

Ingredients:

- 16 oz tempeh, cubed
- 2 tbsp coconut oil
- 1 red bell pepper
- 1 cup snap peas
- 1 cup broccoli

For sauce:

- 3 tbsp peanut butter
- 2 tbsp coconut aminos
- 1 tbsp rice vinegar

- 1 tsp sesame oil
- 1/4 cup water
- 1/2 tsp red pepper flakes

Instructions:

1. Whisk sauce ingredients.
2. Sauté tempeh, then vegetables, and combine with sauce.

Nutrition (per serving):

Calories: 340 | Protein: 31g | Carbs: 18g | Fat: 18g | Fiber: 8g

Substitutions:

Extra-firm tofu | Edamame | Almond butter

Storage:

Refrigerate up to 4 days.

Tip: Steam tempeh before cooking to reduce bitterness.

KEY TAKEAWAYS

- **Prioritize protein at dinner:** Aim for 30–40g per meal to support muscle synthesis.
- **Variety prevents burnout:** Rotate between different protein sources.
- **Prep strategically:** Batch cook proteins for quick assembly.
- **Storage matters:** Proper storage extends freshness and reduces waste.
- **Flexibility is key:** Use substitutions to match preferences.
- **Pair with resistance training:** Protein is most effective with strength exercises.
- **Don't force large portions:** Recipes deliver high protein in manageable servings.
- **Listen to your body:** Choose gentler options if nausea is present.

Chapter 12:
Family-Style Meals

Cooking for a family while on GLP-1 medication doesn't mean preparing two separate dinners. These recipes are crafted to work for everyone at the table - with strategic modifications that let you prioritize protein while others add their preferred carbs or larger portions.

Each recipe provides clear portion guidance: a protein-focused serving for you, and simple add-ons for family members who aren't managing appetite suppression. This approach reduces kitchen stress, saves time, and keeps meals social rather than isolating.

The recipes emphasize lean proteins, fiber-rich vegetables, and flexible scaling. You'll find prep and cook times, full nutrition panels, and storage tips for batch cooking. Icons identify recipes that are quick to prepare, high in protein, gentle on digestion, or plant-based.

These meals are built around the protein-first principle - aiming for 20-35g per serving - while remaining approachable for the whole household. Whether you're feeding kids, a partner, or guests, these dishes deliver flavor and nutrition without requiring you to compromise your goals.

Sheet Pan Lemon Herb Chicken with Roasted Vegetables

◯ High Protein | 👫 Family Friendly

Prep Time: 10 minutes

Cook Time: 30 minutes

Serves: 4 (scales easily)

Why It Works

This one-pan meal delivers 38g of protein per serving with minimal prep. The lean chicken breast supports muscle preservation, while roasted vegetables provide fiber to aid digestion. The simple seasoning is gentle on sensitive stomachs, and the hands-off cooking method reduces kitchen time.

Ingredients

For GLP-1 User (1 serving):

- 6 oz boneless, skinless chicken breast
- 1 cup broccoli florets
- ½ cup sliced bell peppers
- ½ cup zucchini rounds
- 1 tbsp olive oil
- 1 tsp lemon zest
- 1 tsp dried oregano
- ½ tsp garlic powder

- ¼ tsp salt
- Black pepper to taste

For Family (multiply as needed):

- Same base ingredients per person
- Optional add-ons: roasted potatoes, dinner rolls, or cooked quinoa

Instructions

1. Preheat oven to 425°F. Line a large sheet pan with parchment paper.
2. Pat chicken breasts dry and place on one side of the pan.
3. Toss vegetables with olive oil, lemon zest, oregano, garlic powder, salt, and pepper.
4. Arrange vegetables around chicken on the pan.
5. Roast for 25-30 minutes until chicken reaches 165°F internal temperature.
6. Let chicken rest for 5 minutes before slicing.
7. Serve GLP-1 portion with vegetables only; add carbs for family members.

Nutrition (per GLP-1 serving)

- Calories: 310
- Protein: 38g
- Carbohydrates: 12g
- Fiber: 4g
- Fat: 12g
- Sodium: 380mg

Substitutions

- Swap chicken for turkey breast or firm tofu (adjust cook time)
- Use any non-starchy vegetables: asparagus, cauliflower, green beans
- Replace lemon with lime or orange zest

Storage Tips

Refrigerate in airtight containers for up to 4 days. Reheat gently to avoid drying out chicken. Freeze cooked chicken separately from vegetables for up to 3 months.

Tips

Add carbs for family members by roasting cubed sweet potatoes on a separate pan during the last 25 minutes. Keep your portion vegetable-focused to manage fullness.

Slow Cooker Turkey Chili

◯ High Protein | 👨‍👩‍👧 Family Friendly | 🍲 Gentle

Prep Time: 15 minutes

Cook Time: 6 hours (slow cooker)

Serves: 8 (excellent for batch cooking)

Why It Works

Ground turkey provides 32g of lean protein per serving while remaining easy to digest. The slow-cooked texture is gentle on slowed gastric emptying, and the fiber from beans and tomatoes supports satiety. This recipe scales well for meal prep and freezes beautifully.

Ingredients

Base Recipe (8 servings):

- 2 lbs lean ground turkey (93% lean)
- 2 cans (15 oz each) black beans, drained and rinsed
- 1 can (28 oz) crushed tomatoes
- 1 can (14 oz) diced tomatoes
- 1 large onion, diced
- 2 bell peppers, diced
- 3 cloves garlic, minced
- 2 tbsp chili powder
- 1 tbsp cumin
- 1 tsp smoked paprika

- ½ tsp salt
- 2 cups low-sodium chicken broth

For GLP-1 User (1 serving = 1.5 cups):

- Serve as-is

For Family:

- Top with shredded cheese, sour cream, or avocado
- Serve over rice or with cornbread

Instructions

1. Brown ground turkey in a skillet over medium heat, breaking into crumbles. Drain excess fat.
2. Transfer turkey to slow cooker.
3. Add beans, crushed tomatoes, diced tomatoes, onion, bell peppers, garlic, and broth.
4. Stir in chili powder, cumin, paprika, and salt.
5. Cook on low for 6-8 hours or high for 3-4 hours.
6. Stir before serving. Adjust seasoning if needed.

Nutrition (per 1.5-cup serving)

- Calories: 285
- Protein: 32g
- Carbohydrates: 28g
- Fiber: 9g
- Fat: 6g
- Sodium: 420mg

Substitutions

- Use ground chicken or lean beef (90% lean)
- Swap black beans for pinto or kidney beans
- Add diced zucchini or mushrooms for extra vegetables

Storage Tips

Refrigerate for up to 5 days. Freeze in individual portions for up to 4 months. Thaw overnight in the refrigerator before reheating.

Tips

Portion your serving first before adding family toppings. If experiencing nausea, reduce chili powder by half and add mild salsa instead.

Baked Salmon with Green Beans and Almonds

◯ High Protein | 👫 Family Friendly

Prep Time: 8 minutes

Cook Time: 18 minutes

Serves: 4

Why It Works

Salmon delivers 34g of high-quality protein with omega-3 fatty acids that support overall health during weight loss. The mild flavor and tender texture are well-tolerated on GLP-1 medications. Green beans add fiber without heaviness, and almonds provide satisfying crunch.

Ingredients

For GLP-1 User (1 serving):

- 5 oz salmon fillet
- 1½ cups green beans, trimmed
- 1 tbsp sliced almonds
- 1 tsp olive oil
- ½ tsp lemon juice
- ¼ tsp garlic powder
- ¼ tsp salt
- Black pepper to taste

For Family:

- Same base ingredients per person
- Add-on: wild rice, couscous, or roasted potatoes

Instructions

1. Preheat oven to 400°F. Line a baking sheet with foil.
2. Place salmon fillets on one side of the sheet, skin-side down.
3. Toss green beans with olive oil, garlic powder, salt, and pepper.
4. Arrange green beans around salmon.
5. Sprinkle almonds over green beans.
6. Drizzle lemon juice over salmon.
7. Bake for 15-18 minutes until salmon flakes easily with a fork.
8. Serve immediately.

Nutrition (per serving)

- Calories: 295
- Protein: 34g
- Carbohydrates: 9g
- Fiber: 4g
- Fat: 14g
- Sodium: 240mg

Substitutions

- Use trout or Arctic char instead of salmon
- Swap green beans for asparagus or snap peas
- Replace almonds with walnuts or pecans

Storage Tips

Best eaten fresh. Refrigerate leftovers for up to 2 days. Reheat gently at 300°F to prevent drying.

Tips

Family members can add a side of wild rice cooked separately. Keep your plate protein and vegetable-focused to manage portion size.

Greek-Style Turkey Meatballs with Tzatziki

◯ High Protein | 👫 Family Friendly | 🥣 Gentle

Prep Time: 15 minutes

Cook Time: 20 minutes

Serves: 6 (makes 24 meatballs)

Why It Works

These meatballs provide 28g of protein per serving with a soft, moist texture that's easy to digest. The Greek seasoning adds flavor without spice, and the tzatziki sauce offers probiotics from yogurt. Meatballs are portion-controlled and freeze well for quick meals.

Ingredients

Meatballs:

- 2 lbs lean ground turkey
- 1 egg
- ½ cup panko breadcrumbs
- ¼ cup finely chopped fresh parsley
- 3 cloves garlic, minced
- 1 tsp dried oregano
- 1 tsp dried dill
- ½ tsp salt
- ¼ tsp black pepper
- 1 tsp lemon zest

Tzatziki Sauce:

- 1 cup plain Greek yogurt (2% or nonfat)
- ½ cucumber, grated and squeezed dry
- 1 clove garlic, minced
- 1 tbsp fresh dill
- 1 tsp lemon juice
- Pinch of salt

For GLP-1 User (1 serving = 4 meatballs + 3 tbsp tzatziki):

- Serve with cucumber salad or roasted vegetables

For Family:

- Serve over rice, in pita bread, or with pasta

Instructions

1. Preheat oven to 400°F. Line a baking sheet with parchment paper.
2. Combine all meatball ingredients in a large bowl. Mix gently until just combined.
3. Form into 24 meatballs (about 1.5 inches each).
4. Place on prepared baking sheet, spaced evenly.
5. Bake for 18-20 minutes until internal temperature reaches 165°F.
6. While meatballs bake, prepare tzatziki by mixing all sauce ingredients.
7. Serve meatballs with tzatziki on the side.

Nutrition (per serving: 4 meatballs + 3 tbsp tzatziki)

- Calories: 265
- Protein: 28g
- Carbohydrates: 11g
- Fiber: 1g
- Fat: 12g
- Sodium: 380mg

Substitutions

- Use ground chicken instead of turkey
- Replace panko with almond flour for lower carbs
- Swap tzatziki for marinara sauce

Storage Tips

Refrigerate meatballs for up to 4 days. Freeze cooked meatballs for up to 3 months. Store tzatziki separately for up to 3 days.

Tips

Make a double batch and freeze half. Thaw meatballs overnight and reheat for quick protein-first meals during busy weeks.

Vegetarian Lentil Shepherd's Pie

 Family Friendly | 🌿 Plant-Based | 🍲 Gentle

Prep Time: 20 minutes

Cook Time: 35 minutes

Serves: 6

Why It Works

Lentils deliver 22g of plant-based protein per serving with high fiber content that supports digestion and satiety. The mashed cauliflower topping reduces carbs while maintaining comfort-food appeal. This dish is filling for family members but won't overwhelm reduced appetite.

Ingredients

Lentil Base:

- 2 cups cooked green or brown lentils
- 1 tbsp olive oil
- 1 large onion, diced
- 2 carrots, diced
- 2 celery stalks, diced
- 8 oz mushrooms, chopped
- 3 cloves garlic, minced

- 1 can (14 oz) diced tomatoes
- 1 cup low-sodium vegetable broth
- 1 tbsp tomato paste
- 1 tsp dried thyme
- 1 tsp smoked paprika
- ½ tsp salt
- ¼ tsp black pepper

Cauliflower Topping:

- 1 large head cauliflower, cut into florets
- 2 tbsp plain Greek yogurt
- 1 tbsp butter or olive oil
- ¼ tsp garlic powder
- Salt and pepper to taste

For GLP-1 User (1 serving = 1.5 cups):

- Serve as-is

For Family:

- Add shredded cheese on top before baking
- Serve with crusty bread

Instructions

1. Preheat oven to 375°F.
2. Steam cauliflower florets until very tender, about 12 minutes. Drain well.
3. Mash cauliflower with Greek yogurt, butter, garlic powder, salt, and pepper. Set aside.
4. Heat olive oil in a large skillet over medium heat. Sauté onion, carrots, and celery for 5 minutes.
5. Add mushrooms and garlic; cook 3 minutes more.
6. Stir in lentils, diced tomatoes, broth, tomato paste, thyme, paprika, salt, and pepper.
7. Simmer for 10 minutes until thickened.
8. Transfer lentil mixture to a 9x13-inch baking dish.
9. Spread mashed cauliflower evenly over the top.
10. Bake for 25 minutes until lightly golden.
11. Let rest 5 minutes before serving.

Nutrition (per 1.5-cup serving)

- Calories: 245
- Protein: 22g
- Carbohydrates: 35g
- Fiber: 12g
- Fat: 5g
- Sodium: 420mg

Substitutions

- Use sweet potato mash instead of cauliflower for family members
- Add cooked ground turkey to lentil base for extra protein
- Swap lentils for chickpeas

Storage Tips

Refrigerate for up to 4 days. Freeze individual portions for up to 3 months. Reheat covered at 350°F until warmed through.

Tips

Prepare the lentil base and cauliflower topping ahead. Assemble and bake when ready to serve. This reduces same-day cooking time significantly.

Teriyaki Chicken Stir-Fry

◯ High Protein | 👨‍👩‍👧 Family Friendly

Prep Time: 12 minutes

Cook Time: 15 minutes

Serves: 4

Why It Works

This stir-fry provides 35g of protein per serving with colorful vegetables that add fiber and nutrients. The homemade teriyaki sauce controls sodium and sugar while delivering familiar flavors. Quick cooking preserves vegetable texture, making the meal easy to chew and digest.

Ingredients

Teriyaki Sauce:

- 3 tbsp low-sodium soy sauce
- 2 tbsp water
- 1 tbsp rice vinegar
- 1 tbsp honey
- 1 tsp sesame oil
- 1 tsp cornstarch
- 1 clove garlic, minced
- ½ tsp fresh ginger, grated

Stir-Fry:

- 1.5 lbs boneless, skinless chicken breast, cut into 1-inch pieces
- 1 tbsp vegetable oil
- 2 cups broccoli florets
- 1 red bell pepper, sliced
- 1 cup snap peas
- 1 cup sliced mushrooms
- 2 green onions, sliced
- 1 tsp sesame seeds (optional)

For GLP-1 User (1 serving):

- Serve over cauliflower rice or with extra vegetables

For Family:

- Serve over white or brown rice

Instructions

1. Whisk together all teriyaki sauce ingredients in a small bowl. Set aside.
2. Heat vegetable oil in a large skillet or wok over medium-high heat.
3. Add chicken pieces and cook 5-6 minutes until browned and cooked through. Remove and set aside.
4. Add broccoli, bell pepper, snap peas, and mushrooms to the skillet. Stir-fry for 4-5 minutes until crisp-tender.
5. Return chicken to the skillet.
6. Pour teriyaki sauce over chicken and vegetables. Toss to coat.
7. Cook 1-2 minutes until sauce thickens.
8. Garnish with green onions and sesame seeds.

Nutrition (per serving, without rice)

- Calories: 280
- Protein: 35g
- Carbohydrates: 16g
- Fiber: 3g
- Fat: 8g
- Sodium: 480mg

Substitutions

- Use shrimp or tofu instead of chicken
- Swap vegetables based on preference: zucchini, carrots, bok choy
- Replace honey with a sugar substitute if needed

Storage Tips

Refrigerate for up to 3 days. Store rice separately if meal prepping. Reheat gently to avoid overcooking vegetables.

Tips

Prep all ingredients before cooking - stir-fries move quickly. Cook family rice separately so you can control your portion and keep it vegetable-focused.

Baked Cod with Mediterranean Vegetables

◯ High Protein | 👨‍👩‍👧 Family Friendly | 🍲 Gentle

Prep Time: 10 minutes

Cook Time: 25 minutes

Serves: 4

Why It Works

Cod is a lean, mild white fish that provides 30g of protein per serving without heaviness. The flaky texture is gentle on sensitive digestion, and Mediterranean vegetables add fiber and antioxidants. This one-pan meal minimizes cleanup while maximizing nutrition.

Ingredients

For GLP-1 User (1 serving):

- 6 oz cod fillet
- 1 cup cherry tomatoes, halved
- ½ cup diced zucchini
- ½ cup diced yellow squash
- ¼ cup sliced Kalamata olives
- 1 tbsp olive oil
- 1 tsp dried oregano
- 1 clove garlic, minced
- ¼ tsp salt
- Black pepper to taste

- 1 tsp lemon juice
- Fresh parsley for garnish

For Family:

- Same base ingredients per person
- Add-on: couscous, orzo, or crusty bread

Instructions

1. Preheat oven to 400°F. Lightly oil a baking dish.
2. Toss tomatoes, zucchini, squash, and olives with olive oil, oregano, garlic, salt, and pepper.
3. Spread vegetables in the baking dish.
4. Place cod fillets on top of vegetables.
5. Drizzle lemon juice over fish.
6. Bake for 20-25 minutes until fish flakes easily and vegetables are tender.
7. Garnish with fresh parsley.

Nutrition (per serving)

- Calories: 240
- Protein: 30g
- Carbohydrates: 10g
- Fiber: 3g
- Fat: 9g
- Sodium: 380mg

Substitutions

- Use halibut, tilapia, or sea bass instead of cod
- Swap olives for capers
- Add artichoke hearts or roasted red peppers

Storage Tips

Best eaten fresh. Refrigerate leftovers for up to 2 days. Reheat gently at a low temperature to prevent fish from drying out.

Tips

If cod is unavailable, any firm white fish works. Family members can enjoy this over a grain while you focus on the protein and vegetables.

Chicken and White Bean Soup

◯ High Protein | 👨‍👩‍👧 Family Friendly | 🍵 Gentle

Prep Time: 15 minutes

Cook Time: 30 minutes

Serves: 6

Why It Works

This soup delivers 26g of protein per serving from both chicken and white beans. The broth-based format is gentle on slowed digestion, and the soft texture requires minimal chewing. High fiber content from beans supports satiety without causing discomfort.

Ingredients

Base Recipe (6 servings):

- 1 lb boneless, skinless chicken breast
- 1 tbsp olive oil
- 1 large onion, diced
- 3 carrots, sliced
- 3 celery stalks, sliced
- 4 cloves garlic, minced
- 6 cups low-sodium chicken broth
- 2 cans (15 oz each) white beans, drained and rinsed
- 2 cups fresh spinach

- 1 tsp dried thyme
- 1 bay leaf
- ½ tsp salt
- ¼ tsp black pepper
- 1 tbsp lemon juice

For GLP-1 User (1 serving = 1.5 cups):

- Serve as-is

For Family:

- Serve with crusty bread or crackers
- Add pasta for heartier portions

Instructions

1. Heat olive oil in a large pot over medium heat.
2. Add onion, carrots, and celery. Sauté for 5 minutes until softened.
3. Add garlic and cook 1 minute more.
4. Pour in chicken broth. Add chicken breasts, thyme, bay leaf, salt, and pepper.
5. Bring to a boil, then reduce heat and simmer for 20 minutes until chicken is cooked through.
6. Remove chicken, shred with two forks, and return to pot.
7. Add white beans and spinach. Simmer 5 minutes until spinach wilts.
8. Remove bay leaf. Stir in lemon juice before serving.

Nutrition (per 1.5-cup serving)

- Calories: 260
- Protein: 26g
- Carbohydrates: 28g
- Fiber: 8g
- Fat: 5g
- Sodium: 420mg

Substitutions

- Use turkey breast instead of chicken
- Swap white beans for chickpeas or cannellini beans
- Add kale instead of spinach

Storage Tips

Refrigerate for up to 5 days. Freeze for up to 4 months. Thaw overnight in the refrigerator before reheating.

Tips

Make a large batch on weekends for easy weeknight meals. Portion into individual containers for grab-and-go lunches.

Beef and Vegetable Skillet

◯ High Protein | 👫 Family Friendly

Prep Time: 10 minutes

Cook Time: 20 minutes

Serves: 4

Why It Works

Lean ground beef provides 32g of protein per serving with high bioavailability to support muscle preservation. The one-skillet method simplifies cooking, and the vegetable mix adds fiber and volume. This meal is satisfying for the whole family without requiring separate preparations.

Ingredients

For GLP-1 User (1 serving):

- 5 oz lean ground beef (90% lean)
- 1 cup riced cauliflower
- ½ cup diced bell peppers
- ½ cup diced zucchini
- ¼ cup diced onion
- 2 cloves garlic, minced
- ½ cup diced tomatoes
- 1 tsp olive oil
- 1 tsp Italian seasoning

- ¼ tsp salt
- Black pepper to taste
- 1 tbsp grated Parmesan cheese

For Family:

- Same base ingredients per person
- Add-on: serve over pasta or rice

Instructions

1. Heat olive oil in a large skillet over medium-high heat.
2. Add ground beef and cook 5-6 minutes, breaking into crumbles, until browned. Drain excess fat.
3. Add onion, bell peppers, and zucchini. Cook 4 minutes until softened.
4. Stir in garlic and cook 1 minute.
5. Add riced cauliflower, diced tomatoes, Italian seasoning, salt, and pepper.
6. Cook 5-7 minutes, stirring occasionally, until vegetables are tender.
7. Sprinkle with Parmesan cheese before serving.

Nutrition (per serving)

- Calories: 295
- Protein: 32g
- Carbohydrates: 12g
- Fiber: 4g
- Fat: 14g
- Sodium: 340mg

Substitutions

- Use ground turkey or chicken instead of beef
- Swap riced cauliflower for regular rice (for family members)
- Add mushrooms or spinach for extra vegetables

Storage Tips

Refrigerate for up to 4 days. Reheat in a skillet over medium heat, adding a splash of water if needed.

Tips

Double the recipe and freeze half for quick future meals. Family members can add their preferred grain while you keep your portion vegetable-focused.

Tofu and Vegetable Curry

 Family Friendly |  Plant-Based | Gentle

Prep Time: 15 minutes

Cook Time: 25 minutes

Serves: 5

Why It Works

Firm tofu provides 24g of plant-based protein per serving with a soft texture that's easy to digest. The curry sauce is flavorful but not overly spicy, and coconut milk adds healthy fats that support nutrient absorption. This dish is naturally gentle on sensitive stomachs.

Ingredients

Base Recipe (5 servings):

- 1 block (14 oz) extra-firm tofu, pressed and cubed
- 1 tbsp coconut oil
- 1 large onion, diced
- 3 cloves garlic, minced
- 1 tbsp fresh ginger, grated
- 2 tbsp mild curry powder
- 1 can (14 oz) light coconut milk
- 1 cup low-sodium vegetable broth
- 2 cups cauliflower florets

- 1 red bell pepper, sliced
- 1 cup green beans, trimmed and halved
- 1 cup diced tomatoes
- 1 tbsp tomato paste
- ½ tsp salt
- 1 tbsp lime juice
- Fresh cilantro for garnish

For GLP-1 User (1 serving = 1.5 cups):

- Serve over cauliflower rice

For Family:

- Serve over basmati or jasmine rice

Instructions

1. Heat coconut oil in a large pot over medium heat.
2. Add onion and cook 4 minutes until softened.
3. Stir in garlic, ginger, and curry powder. Cook 1 minute until fragrant.
4. Pour in coconut milk and vegetable broth.
5. Add cauliflower, bell pepper, green beans, diced tomatoes, tomato paste, and salt.
6. Bring to a simmer and cook 12 minutes until vegetables are tender.
7. Gently fold in tofu cubes. Simmer 5 minutes more.
8. Remove from heat and stir in lime juice.
9. Garnish with fresh cilantro.

Nutrition (per 1.5-cup serving)

- Calories: 270
- Protein: 24g
- Carbohydrates: 18g
- Fiber: 6g
- Fat: 13g
- Sodium: 380mg

Substitutions

- Use chickpeas instead of tofu
- Swap green beans for snap peas or broccoli
- Replace coconut milk with cashew cream for a nut-based option

Storage Tips

Refrigerate for up to 4 days. Freeze for up to 3 months. Store rice separately if meal prepping.

Tips

Press tofu well before cubing to improve texture. If curry is too thick after refrigeration, add a splash of broth when reheating.

Key Takeaways

- Family-style meals can accommodate GLP-1 users and non-users with simple portion adjustments and add-on carbs.
- Prioritize protein-first servings of 20-35g to support muscle preservation during weight loss.
- One-pan and slow cooker recipes reduce kitchen time while delivering nutrient-dense meals.
- Batch cooking and freezing portions ensures quick access to balanced meals during busy weeks.
- Mild seasonings and soft textures support digestion when gastric emptying is slowed.
- Scaling recipes allows flexibility—cook once, serve multiple portions, and store extras efficiently.
- Plant-based options like lentils and tofu provide high protein and fiber without animal products.
- Clear portion guidance prevents overeating while keeping meals social and inclusive.

Chapter 13:
Small Plates & Snack Meals

When appetite dwindles, meal structure must adapt. GLP-1 medications delay gastric emptying and curb hunger, making it challenging to follow traditional three-meal patterns. Many find themselves unintentionally skipping meals because a full plate seems daunting.

This leads to a nutritional challenge: the body requires sufficient protein and nutrients to preserve muscle mass during weight loss, yet eating feels burdensome. The solution isn't to force large meals but to rethink how you eat.

Small plates and snack-style meals offer a way to meet protein needs without inducing fullness or nausea. These recipes focus on nutrient density in compact portions, each providing 15–25 grams of protein in formats suitable for reduced appetite: soft textures, mild flavors, and quick preparation.

These aren't typical snacks; they're strategic meals for when eating feels difficult. Use them as main meals, protein boosts between meals, or lighter alternatives to heavy dinners. The goal is consistent protein intake, even when hunger is absent.

Mediterranean Protein Bento Box

Prep time: 8 minutes

Cook time: 0 minutes

Servings: 1

Why It Works

Bento-style eating minimizes decision fatigue and portion stress. Each mild, protein-rich component is easy to digest. The variety prevents flavor fatigue while delivering balanced nutrition in a visually pleasant format.

Ingredients

- 3 oz grilled chicken breast, sliced thin
- ¼ cup hummus
- 10 cucumber slices
- 8 cherry tomatoes, halved
- 2 oz feta cheese, cubed
- 6 Kalamata olives
- 1 small whole wheat pita, cut into triangles

Instructions

1. Arrange chicken slices in one section of a divided container.
2. Place hummus in another section.
3. Group cucumber, tomatoes, feta, and olives.
4. Serve pita on the side or toasted.
5. Enjoy components separately or combined.

Nutrition (per serving)

- **Calories**: 425
- **Protein**: 38g
- **Carbohydrates**: 28g
- **Fat:** 18g
- **Fiber:** 6g
- **Sodium:** 890mg

Substitutions

- Swap chicken for canned tuna or hard-boiled eggs.
- Use tzatziki instead of hummus for fewer calories.
- Replace pita with rice crackers for gluten-free.

Storage

Store components separately for up to 3 days. Keep pita separate to prevent sogginess.

Tip: Prep three boxes on Sunday for easy meals throughout the week.

Greek Yogurt Power Bowl

⏱ Quick | ◯ High Protein | 🥣 Gentle

Prep time: 5 minutes

Cook time: 0 minutes

Servings: 1

Why It Works

Yogurt's smooth texture and mild taste suit suppressed appetites. Protein powder enhances content without bulk. Toppings add texture and nutrients in small bites.

Ingredients

- 1 cup plain Greek yogurt (2% or full-fat)
- 1 scoop vanilla protein powder
- 2 tbsp sliced almonds
- ¼ cup blueberries
- 1 tsp honey
- Pinch of cinnamon

Instructions

1. Blend protein powder with yogurt until smooth.
2. Transfer to a bowl.
3. Top with almonds and blueberries.
4. Drizzle honey and dust with cinnamon.
5. Serve immediately.

Nutrition (per serving)

- Calories: 380
- Protein: 42g
- Carbohydrates: 32g
- Fat: 10g
- Fiber: 3g
- Sodium: 140mg

Substitutions

- Use unflavored protein powder and add vanilla extract.
- Swap almonds for walnuts or pumpkin seeds.
- Replace blueberries with strawberries or raspberries.

Storage

Mix yogurt and protein powder up to 2 days in advance. Add toppings just before eating.

Tip: If too thick, thin with 1–2 tablespoons of milk.

Egg Salad Lettuce Cups

🕛 Quick | 🥚 High Protein | 🍯 Gentle | 🌿 Plant-Based Option

Prep time: 10 minutes

Cook time: 0 minutes (using pre-cooked eggs)

Servings: 1

Why It Works

Eggs offer complete protein in a soft, digestible format. Lettuce cups eliminate bread bulk while adding a satisfying crunch.

Ingredients

- 3 hard-boiled eggs, chopped
- 2 tbsp plain Greek yogurt
- 1 tsp Dijon mustard
- 1 tbsp finely diced celery
- 1 tsp fresh dill, chopped
- Salt and pepper to taste
- 4 large butter lettuce leaves

Instructions

1. Mix chopped eggs, yogurt, mustard, celery, and dill.
2. Season with salt and pepper.
3. Divide mixture among lettuce leaves.
4. Serve immediately or refrigerate.

Nutrition (per serving)

- Calories: 295
- Protein: 24g
- Carbohydrates: 5g
- Fat: 19g
- Fiber: 1g
- Sodium: 320mg

Substitutions

- Use mayonnaise instead of Greek yogurt for richer flavor.
- Replace dill with chives or parsley.
- Try romaine or endive instead of butter lettuce.

Storage

Egg salad keeps for 3 days refrigerated. Store separately from lettuce.

Tip: Make a double batch for quick meals throughout the week.

Turkey & Cheese Roll-Ups

⏱ Quick | ◯ High Protein | 👩‍👧 Family Friendly

Prep time: 5 minutes

Cook time: 0 minutes

Servings: 1

Why It Works

No cooking, no utensils, no bulk. Roll-ups deliver concentrated protein without the weight of bread.

Ingredients

- 4 slices deli turkey breast (low sodium)
- 2 slices Swiss cheese
- 2 tbsp hummus or cream cheese
- 4 thin cucumber spears
- 4 roasted red pepper strips

Instructions

1. Lay turkey slices flat.
2. Spread hummus on each slice.
3. Add a half slice of cheese, a cucumber spear, and a pepper strip.
4. Roll tightly and secure with a toothpick if needed.
5. Serve immediately or refrigerate.

Nutrition (per serving)

- Calories: 285
- Protein: 32g
- Carbohydrates: 8g
- Fat: 13g
- Fiber: 2g
- Sodium: 780mg

Substitutions

- Use chicken or ham instead of turkey.
- Try provolone or cheddar instead of Swiss.
- Replace cucumber with avocado slices.

Storage

Assemble up to 1 day ahead. Store wrapped in parchment paper.

Tip: Pair with a small handful of grapes for a complete portable meal.

Cottage Cheese Protein Plate

Quick | High Protein | Gentle

Prep time: 5 minutes

Cook time: 0 minutes

Servings: 1

Why It Works

Cottage cheese provides slow-digesting casein protein in a mild format. Fruit and nuts create a balanced macro profile without overwhelming volume.

Ingredients

- 1 cup cottage cheese (2% or 4%)
- ½ cup pineapple chunks (fresh or canned in juice)
- 2 tbsp chopped walnuts
- 1 tsp chia seeds
- Drizzle of honey (optional)

Instructions

1. Place cottage cheese in a bowl.
2. Top with pineapple, walnuts, and chia seeds.
3. Add honey if desired.
4. Serve immediately.

Nutrition (per serving)

- Calories: 340
- Protein: 30g
- Carbohydrates: 26g
- Fat: 13g
- Fiber: 3g
- Sodium: 680mg

Substitutions

- Use peaches or berries instead of pineapple.
- Replace walnuts with almonds or pecans.
- Try hemp seeds instead of chia.

Storage

Store cottage cheese and toppings separately for up to 3 days.

Tip: Blend cottage cheese until smooth if texture is off-putting.

Tuna Avocado Boats

⏱ Quick | ◯ High Protein | 🥣 Gentle

Prep time: 7 minutes

Cook time: 0 minutes

Servings: 1

Why It Works

Tuna provides complete protein with minimal prep. Avocado adds healthy fats and a creamy texture without cooking.

Ingredients

- 1 can (5 oz) tuna in water, drained
- 1 ripe avocado, halved and pitted
- 1 tbsp plain Greek yogurt
- 1 tsp lemon juice
- 1 tbsp diced red onion
- Salt and pepper to taste
- Cherry tomatoes for garnish

Instructions

1. Scoop small amount of avocado to create a deeper well.
2. Mash scooped avocado with tuna, yogurt, and lemon juice.
3. Stir in red onion.
4. Season with salt and pepper.
5. Divide mixture between avocado halves.
6. Garnish with cherry tomatoes.

Nutrition (per serving)

- Calories: 395
- Protein: 35g
- Carbohydrates: 14g
- Fat: 23g
- Fiber: 10g
- Sodium: 380mg

Substitutions

- Use canned salmon instead of tuna.
- Replace Greek yogurt with mayonnaise.
- Add diced cucumber for crunch.

Storage

Best eaten immediately. Tuna mixture can be stored 1 day; fill avocado just before serving.

Tip: Squeeze extra lemon juice on avocado to prevent browning.

Protein-Packed Hummus Plate

🕐 Quick | 🌿 Plant-Based | 🥣 Gentle

Prep time: 8 minutes

Cook time: 0 minutes

Servings: 1

Why It Works

Plant-based protein from chickpeas and edamame delivers a complete amino acid profile. The variety keeps portions manageable and textures interesting.

Ingredients

- ½ cup hummus
- ½ cup shelled edamame, cooked and cooled
- 1 mini cucumber, sliced
- 1 medium carrot, cut into sticks
- 6 whole grain crackers
- 2 tbsp sunflower seeds

Instructions

1. Place hummus in the center of a plate.
2. Arrange edamame, cucumber, and carrot around it.
3. Add crackers to the side.
4. Sprinkle sunflower seeds over hummus.
5. Serve immediately.

Nutrition (per serving)

- Calories: 420
- Protein: 21g
- Carbohydrates: 42g
- Fat: 19g
- Fiber: 13g
- Sodium: 520mg

Substitutions

- Use white beans instead of edamame.
- Replace crackers with pita chips.
- Try pumpkin seeds instead of sunflower seeds.

Storage

Store components separately for up to 3 days. Assemble before eating.

Tip: Add 2 tablespoons of hemp hearts to boost protein to 27g.

Mini Caprese Skewers with Chicken

⏱ Quick | ◯ High Protein | 👭 Family Friendly

Prep time: 10 minutes

Cook time: 0 minutes

Servings: 1 (6 skewers)

Why It Works

Skewers transform eating into a low-pressure activity. Each bite is perfectly portioned, encouraging slow eating and fullness awareness.

Ingredients

- 3 oz grilled chicken breast, cut into cubes
- 12 cherry tomatoes
- 12 small mozzarella balls (ciliegine)
- 12 fresh basil leaves
- 1 tbsp balsamic glaze
- 6 small skewers or toothpicks

Instructions

1. Thread each skewer with chicken, basil, tomato, and mozzarella.
2. Repeat pattern once per skewer.
3. Arrange on plate.
4. Drizzle with balsamic glaze.
5. Serve immediately or refrigerate up to 4 hours.

Nutrition (per serving)

- Calories: 310
- Protein: 35g
- Carbohydrates: 12g
- Fat: 13g
- Fiber: 2g
- Sodium: 420mg

Substitutions

- Use turkey instead of chicken.
- Replace mozzarella with feta.
- Try pesto instead of balsamic glaze.

Storage

Assemble up to 4 hours ahead. Store in refrigerator.

Tip: Make extra for everyone—these disappear quickly.

Smoked Salmon Cucumber Rounds

🕐 Quick | ◯ High Protein | 🥣 Gentle

Prep time: 8 minutes

Cook time: 0 minutes

Servings: 1 (8 rounds)

Why It Works

Salmon provides omega-3 fatty acids and complete protein in a delicate format. Cucumber keeps the meal light while cream cheese adds richness.

Ingredients

- 1 large cucumber, cut into rounds
- 3 oz smoked salmon, torn into pieces
- 3 tbsp whipped cream cheese
- 1 tsp capers
- Fresh dill for garnish
- Lemon wedge

Instructions

1. Pat cucumber rounds dry.
2. Spread cream cheese on each.
3. Top with salmon.
4. Add capers to each.

5. Garnish with dill.

6. Serve with lemon wedge.

Nutrition (per serving)

- Calories: 220
- Protein: 20g
- Carbohydrates: 8g
- Fat: 12g
- Fiber: 1g
- Sodium: 980mg

Substitutions

- Use canned salmon instead of smoked.
- Replace cream cheese with Greek yogurt.
- Try radish slices instead of cucumber.

Storage

Best assembled fresh. Prep components 1 day ahead.

Tip: Use English cucumber for less watery rounds.

Peanut Butter Banana Protein Bites

⏱ Quick | ◯ High Protein | 👫 Family Friendly | 🍲 Gentle

Prep time: 5 minutes

Cook time: 0 minutes

Servings: 1 (6 bites)

Why It Works

Sweet flavors can entice when savory foods don't appeal. The blend of protein, healthy fats, and natural sugars offers sustained energy in a familiar format.

Ingredients

- 1 medium banana, cut into rounds
- 3 tbsp natural peanut butter
- 2 tbsp vanilla protein powder
- 1 tbsp mini chocolate chips
- Pinch of sea salt

Instructions

1. Mix peanut butter and protein powder until smooth.
2. Spread on banana rounds.
3. Sprinkle with chocolate chips.
4. Add a pinch of sea salt.
5. Serve immediately or refrigerate for firmer texture.

Nutrition (per serving)

- Calories: 395
- Protein: 22g
- Carbohydrates: 38g
- Fat: 18g
- Fiber: 6g
- Sodium: 180mg

Substitutions

- Use almond butter instead of peanut butter.
- Replace chocolate chips with nuts.
- Try apple slices instead of banana.

Storage

Best eaten fresh. Refrigerate up to 4 hours but banana may brown.

Tip: Freeze for 1 hour for a dessert-like texture.

White Bean & Tuna Salad Cup

⏱ Quick | ◯ High Protein | 🥣 Gentle

Prep time: 8 minutes

Cook time: 0 minutes

Servings: 1

Why It Works

Beans add fiber and plant protein, while tuna offers complete amino acids. The soft texture requires minimal chewing.

Ingredients

- 1 can (5 oz) tuna in water, drained
- ½ cup canned white beans, rinsed
- 2 tbsp diced red bell pepper
- 1 tbsp olive oil
- 1 tbsp lemon juice
- 1 tsp Dijon mustard
- 2 cups mixed greens
- Salt and pepper to taste

Instructions

1. Combine tuna, beans, and bell pepper.
2. Whisk olive oil, lemon juice, and mustard.
3. Pour over tuna mixture and toss.
4. Season with salt and pepper.
5. Serve over greens or eat directly from bowl.

Nutrition (per serving)

- Calories: 360
- Protein: 38g
- Carbohydrates: 22g
- Fat: 15g
- Fiber: 7g
- Sodium: 480mg

Substitutions

- Use chickpeas instead of white beans.
- Replace tuna with canned chicken.
- Add diced cucumber for crunch.

Storage

Tuna mixture keeps 2 days refrigerated. Store separately from greens.

Tip: Mash beans slightly for creamier texture.

Egg & Veggie Muffin Cups

⏱ Quick | 🥚 High Protein | 👫 Family Friendly

Prep time: 10 minutes

Cook time: 18 minutes

Servings: 6 muffins (serving = 2 muffins)

Why It Works

Pre-portioned egg cups simplify decision-making and provide grab-and-go protein. Vegetables add nutrients without bulk.

Ingredients

- 6 large eggs
- ¼ cup milk
- ½ cup diced bell peppers
- ¼ cup diced onion
- ½ cup shredded cheddar cheese
- 2 cups fresh spinach, chopped
- Salt and pepper to taste
- Cooking spray

Instructions

1. Preheat oven to 350°F. Spray muffin tin.
2. Whisk eggs and milk.
3. Stir in peppers, onion, cheese, and spinach.
4. Season with salt and pepper.
5. Divide among muffin cups.
6. Bake 18 minutes until set.
7. Cool before removing.

Nutrition (per serving - 2 muffins)

- Calories: 280
- Protein: 22g
- Carbohydrates: 6g
- Fat: 18g
- Fiber: 1g
- Sodium: 380mg

Substitutions

- Use any vegetables you tolerate well.
- Replace cheddar with feta or Swiss.
- Add turkey sausage for extra protein.

Storage

Refrigerate up to 5 days. Freeze up to 2 months. Reheat in microwave.

Tip: Make a full batch for easy breakfasts or snacks.

Chicken & Veggie Lettuce Wraps

🕐 Quick | ◯ High Protein | 🥣 Gentle

Prep time: 10 minutes

Cook time: 0 minutes (using pre-cooked chicken)

Servings: 1 (3 wraps)

Why It Works

Lettuce wraps eliminate the bulk of bread while providing satisfying crunch. Asian-inspired flavors can boost appetite when other foods don't appeal.

Ingredients

- 4 oz cooked chicken breast, shredded
- 1 tbsp low-sodium soy sauce
- 1 tsp rice vinegar
- ½ tsp sesame oil
- ¼ cup shredded carrot
- ¼ cup diced cucumber
- 2 tbsp chopped peanuts
- 3 large butter lettuce leaves
- Lime wedge

Instructions

1. Mix chicken with soy sauce, vinegar, and sesame oil.
2. Add carrot and cucumber.
3. Divide among lettuce leaves.
4. Top with peanuts.
5. Serve with lime wedge.

Nutrition (per serving)

- Calories: 295
- Protein: 35g
- Carbohydrates: 10g
- Fat: 12g
- Fiber: 3g
- Sodium: 520mg

Substitutions

- Use ground turkey instead of chicken.
- Replace peanuts with cashews or almonds.
- Try napa cabbage instead of lettuce.

Storage

Store filling separately for up to 2 days.

Tip: Add sriracha mayo for extra flavor.

Protein Smoothie Bowl

⏱ Quick | ⬡ High Protein | 🥣 Gentle | 🌿 Plant-Based Option

Prep time: 5 minutes

Cook time: 0 minutes

Servings: 1

Why It Works

Smoothie bowls provide complete nutrition in an easy-to-consume format. The cold and smooth texture is gentle on the stomach.

Ingredients

- 1 cup unsweetened almond milk
- 1 scoop vanilla protein powder
- ½ cup frozen mixed berries
- ½ frozen banana
- 2 tbsp Greek yogurt
- Toppings: 1 tbsp granola, 1 tbsp sliced almonds, 5 blueberries

Instructions

1. Blend almond milk, protein powder, berries, banana, and yogurt until smooth.
2. Pour into a bowl.
3. Arrange toppings.
4. Serve immediately.

Nutrition (per serving)

- Calories: 350
- Protein: 32g
- Carbohydrates: 38g
- Fat: 9g
- Fiber: 7g
- Sodium: 240mg

Substitutions

- Use any milk you prefer.
- Replace berries with mango or peach.
- Try chia seeds instead of granola.

Storage

Blend base and refrigerate up to 4 hours.

Tip: Add nut butter for extra calories and richness.

Quick Protein Quesadilla

⏱ Quick | ◯ High Protein | 👨‍👩‍👧 Family Friendly

Prep time: 5 minutes

Cook time: 6 minutes

Servings: 1

Why It Works

This comfort food is optimized for protein. The warm, cheesy tortilla is more appealing than cold foods when appetite is low.

Ingredients

- 1 whole wheat tortilla
- 3 oz cooked chicken breast, diced
- ⅓ cup shredded Mexican cheese blend
- 2 tbsp black beans, rinsed
- 1 tbsp salsa
- Cooking spray
- Optional: Greek yogurt for serving

Instructions

1. Spray skillet with cooking spray and heat over medium.
2. Lay tortilla in pan.
3. Add cheese, chicken, beans, and salsa on half of tortilla.

4. Fold tortilla in half.

5. Cook 3 minutes per side until golden.

6. Cut into triangles.

7. Serve with Greek yogurt if desired.

Nutrition (per serving)

- Calories: 380
- Protein: 36g
- Carbohydrates: 28g
- Fat: 14g
- Fiber: 5g
- Sodium: 680mg

Substitutions

- Use ground turkey instead of chicken.
- Replace black beans with pinto beans.
- Try whole grain wrap for different texture.

Storage

Best eaten fresh. Refrigerate 1 day and reheat in skillet.

Tip: Add mashed avocado before folding for extra creaminess.

Common Mistakes to Avoid

Skipping meals because you're not hungry. Appetite suppression doesn't eliminate protein needs. Use these small plates to maintain intake even when hunger is absent.

Waiting until you're extremely hungry. Delayed gastric emptying means meals take longer to digest. Eat before true hunger hits to avoid nausea.

Choosing only sweet or only savory options. Rotate flavor profiles to prevent taste fatigue and maintain interest in eating.

Ignoring texture preferences. If certain textures trigger nausea, avoid them. These recipes offer variety - use what works for your body.

Not preparing ahead. Low appetite often coincides with low motivation. Batch prep components on good days for easy assembly later.

Forcing large portions. These recipes are designed as complete small meals. Don't feel obligated to eat more than feels comfortable.

- Small plates deliver adequate protein without overwhelming reduced appetite.
- Each recipe provides 20–38 grams of protein in manageable portions.
- Prepare components in advance for low-effort assembly on difficult days.
- Rotate between textures and flavors to maintain eating consistency.
- Cold and room-temperature options work well when hot foods feel heavy.
- Bento-style meals and hand-held formats reduce eating pressure.
- Use these as primary meals, not just snacks, when appetite is suppressed.
- Storage guidance allows batch preparation for multiple days of easy meals.

Chapter 14:
Nausea-Friendly & Gentle Meals

When nausea strikes, eating can feel like a challenge. GLP-1 medications slow gastric emptying and enhance the feeling of fullness, often leading to queasiness, especially during dose increases or after rich meals.

The key isn't to stop eating - it's to eat wisely. Gentle meals are easy to digest, low in fat, and mild in flavor. They prevent overwhelming your system or triggering nausea. These recipes emphasize simple carbohydrates, lean proteins, and minimal seasoning while still providing necessary nutrients to preserve muscle and maintain energy.

Each recipe is crafted to be tolerable when appetite is low. They're soft and portion-controlled, suitable for any time of day. Light broths, soft rice bowls, and toast-based meals offer practical ways to manage GLP-1 side effects while maintaining protein intake.

Use these recipes during flare-ups, after dose increases, or whenever you need something that won't fight back.

Ginger Chicken Rice Bowl

Quick | High Protein | Gentle

Prep time: 5 minutes

Cook time: 15 minutes

Serves: 1

Why It Works

White rice is easily digestible, while ginger soothes nausea. Shredded chicken provides lean protein without heavy textures. This bowl is mild and simple, perfect for when nutrition is essential but bold flavors are not.

Ingredients

- ½ cup white rice (uncooked)
- 3 oz cooked chicken breast, shredded
- 1 cup low-sodium chicken broth
- 1 tsp fresh ginger, grated
- ¼ tsp salt
- 1 tsp sesame oil (optional)
- 1 tbsp green onion, finely chopped (optional)

Instructions

1. Cook rice according to package directions using chicken broth.
2. Warm shredded chicken in a pan with ginger and a splash of broth.
3. Fluff rice, transfer to a bowl, and top with chicken mixture.
4. Drizzle with sesame oil and garnish with green onion if desired.

Nutrition (per serving)

- Calories: 320
- Protein: 28g
- Carbs: 42g
- Fat: 3g
- Fiber: 1g
- Sodium: 480mg

Substitutions

- Use rotisserie chicken for convenience
- Swap chicken for tofu (protein ~18g)
- Use jasmine or basmati rice for softer texture

Storage

Refrigerate up to 3 days. Reheat with a splash of broth.

Tip: Adjust ginger to taste or omit if too strong.

Simple Bone Broth with Soft Egg

⏱ Quick | ◯ High Protein | 🍲 Gentle

Prep time: 2 minutes

Cook time: 8 minutes

Serves: 1

Why It Works

Bone broth is hydrating and full of electrolytes. A soft-boiled egg provides high-quality protein, making this a gentle and easy-to-sip meal.

Ingredients

- 1½ cups bone broth (chicken or beef)
- 1 large egg
- Pinch of salt
- ¼ tsp white pepper (optional)
- 1 tsp fresh parsley, chopped (optional)

Instructions

1. Simmer bone broth in a small pot.
2. Soft-boil the egg (6–7 minutes) and cool in ice water.
3. Peel and slice the egg.
4. Pour hot broth into a bowl, add egg halves, and season with salt, pepper, and parsley.

Nutrition (per serving)

- Calories: 110
- Protein: 12g
- Carbs: 2g
- Fat: 6g
- Sodium: 620mg

Substitutions

- Use store-bought bone broth (check sodium)
- Add cooked rice noodles for extra carbs
- Use a poached egg instead

Storage

Broth keeps 5 days refrigerated. Prepare egg fresh.

Tip: Start with broth alone if nausea is severe.

Miso Tofu Soup

⏱ Quick | 🌿 Plant-Based | 🍲 Gentle

Prep time: 5 minutes

Cook time: 10 minutes

Serves: 1

Why It Works

Miso is fermented and easy on digestion. Silken tofu offers soft, protein-rich sustenance, making this soup warming and easy to digest.

Ingredients

- 1½ cups water
- 2 tbsp white miso paste
- 4 oz silken tofu, cubed
- 1 tbsp wakame seaweed (dried)
- 1 tsp green onion, sliced
- ¼ tsp ginger powder (optional)

Instructions

- Heat water until steaming, then dissolve miso paste.
- Add tofu and wakame, simmering gently for 3–4 minutes.
- Remove from heat and garnish with green onion.

Nutrition (per serving)

- Calories: 130
- Protein: 12g
- Carbs: 10g
- Fat: 5g
- Fiber: 2g
- Sodium: 780mg

Substitutions

- Use firm tofu if needed (less soft texture)
- Omit wakame if unappealing
- Add soba noodles for more substance

Storage

Best fresh. Miso may separate when reheated.

Tip: Start with 1 tbsp miso if sensitive to salt.

Plain Scrambled Eggs on Toast

⏱ Quick | ◯ High Protein | 🥣 Gentle

Prep time: 3 minutes

Cook time: 5 minutes

Serves: 1

Why It Works

Scrambled eggs are soft and protein-rich, paired with white toast for simple carbs that calm the stomach.

Ingredients

- 2 large eggs
- 1 tsp butter or olive oil
- 1 slice white bread, toasted
- Pinch of salt

Instructions

1. Whisk eggs with salt.
2. Heat butter in a nonstick pan, then cook eggs gently until set.
3. Serve over toasted bread.

Nutrition (per serving)

- Calories: 250
- Protein: 15g
- Carbs: 14g
- Fat: 14g
- Fiber: 1g
- Sodium: 320mg

Substitutions

- Use different bread types (digestibility varies)
- Add shredded cheese for extra protein
- Use egg whites to reduce fat

Storage

Consume fresh. Eggs become rubbery when reheated.

Tip: Low heat cooking makes eggs easier to digest.

Banana Oat Smoothie

⏱ Quick | 🥣 Gentle | 👨‍👩‍👧 Family Friendly

Prep time: 3 minutes

Cook time: 0 minutes

Serves: 1

Why It Works

Bananas are gentle on the stomach, oats add thickness, and Greek yogurt provides protein. This smoothie is smooth and easy on the palate.

Ingredients

- 1 small ripe banana
- ¼ cup rolled oats
- ½ cup plain Greek yogurt (2%)
- ½ cup unsweetened almond milk
- ½ tsp vanilla extract
- 3–4 ice cubes

Instructions

1. Blend all ingredients until smooth.
2. Pour into a glass and sip slowly.

Nutrition (per serving)

- Calories: 260
- Protein: 16g
- Carbs: 40g
- Fat: 4g
- Fiber: 5g
- Sodium: 90mg

Substitutions

- Use regular yogurt for a thinner consistency
- Swap almond milk with oat or skim milk
- Add peanut butter for more protein

Storage

Best fresh. Smoothies separate if stored.

Tip: Sip over 20–30 minutes to ease digestion.

Plain Chicken & Rice Soup

⏱ Quick | ◯ High Protein | 🍲 Gentle | 👪 Family Friendly

Prep time: 5 minutes

Cook time: 20 minutes

Serves: 2

Why It Works

A classic comfort dish, this soup combines easy-to-digest rice and chicken in a mild broth, providing warmth and hydration.

Ingredients

- 3 cups low-sodium chicken broth
- ½ cup white rice (uncooked)
- 4 oz cooked chicken breast, shredded
- ¼ tsp salt
- ¼ tsp black pepper (optional)
- 1 tbsp fresh parsley, chopped (optional)

Instructions

1. Bring broth to a boil, add rice, and simmer.
2. Cook until rice is tender, then add chicken.
3. Season and garnish with parsley.

Nutrition (per serving)

- Calories: 210
- Protein: 18g
- Carbs: 28g
- Fat: 2g
- Fiber: 1g
- Sodium: 520mg

Substitutions

- Use rotisserie chicken for ease
- Swap rice for pasta (cook time varies)
- Add carrots for extra nutrients

Storage

Refrigerate up to 4 days. Add broth when reheating.

Tip: Double the recipe and freeze portions for later.

Applesauce & Cottage Cheese Bowl

⏱ Quick | ◯ High Protein | 🥣 Gentle

Prep time: 2 minutes

Cook time: 0 minutes

Serves: 1

Why It Works

Applesauce is naturally sweet and easy to digest, while cottage cheese provides protein without requiring chewing.

Ingredients

- ½ cup unsweetened applesauce
- ½ cup low-fat cottage cheese (2%)
- 1 tsp honey (optional)
- Pinch of cinnamon (optional)

Instructions

1. Spoon cottage cheese into a bowl and top with applesauce.
2. Drizzle with honey and sprinkle with cinnamon if desired.

Nutrition (per serving)

- Calories: 160
- Protein: 16g

- Carbs: 20g
- Fat: 2g
- Fiber: 2g
- Sodium: 380mg

Substitutions

- Substitute cottage cheese with Greek yogurt
- Swap applesauce for mashed banana
- Use full-fat cottage cheese for extra calories

Storage

Consume fresh. Can assemble a day ahead.

Tip: Enjoy cold for better tolerance.

Plain Baked Potato with Greek Yogurt

⏱ Quick | 🍲 Gentle | 🌿 Plant-Based (if modified)

Prep time: 2 minutes

Cook time: 8 minutes (microwave)

Serves: 1

Why It Works

Baked potatoes provide mild starches and satiety, while Greek yogurt adds protein and creaminess without excess fat.

Ingredients

- 1 medium russet potato
- ¼ cup plain Greek yogurt (2%)
- Pinch of salt
- 1 tsp chives, chopped (optional)

Instructions

1. Microwave potato until soft, pierce with a fork.
2. Slice open and fluff. Top with yogurt, salt, and chives.

Nutrition (per serving)

- Calories: 220
- Protein: 10g

- Carbs: 42g
- Fat: 1g
- Fiber: 4g
- Sodium: 180mg

Substitutions

- Use sweet potato for added nutrients
- Swap yogurt for cottage cheese
- Add chicken for extra protein

Storage

Refrigerate baked potatoes for up to 3 days.

Tip: Keep toppings minimal with severe nausea.

Rice Pudding with Cinnamon

⏱ Quick | 🍲 Gentle | 👨‍👩‍👧 Family Friendly

Prep time: 2 minutes

Cook time: 20 minutes

Serves: 2

Why It Works

Soft and mildly sweet, rice pudding comforts while milk adds protein. Cinnamon helps soothe digestion.

Ingredients

- ½ cup white rice (uncooked)
- 1½ cups 2% milk
- 2 tbsp sugar
- ½ tsp vanilla extract
- ¼ tsp cinnamon
- Pinch of salt

Instructions

1. Combine rice, milk, sugar, and salt in a pot.
2. Simmer, stirring frequently, until rice is tender.
3. Stir in vanilla and cinnamon.

Nutrition (per serving)

- Calories: 240
- Protein: 8g
- Carbs: 45g
- Fat: 3g
- Fiber: 1g
- Sodium: 110mg

Substitutions

- Use almond or oat milk (lower protein)
- Replace sugar with honey
- Add raisins for sweetness

Storage

Refrigerate up to 4 days. Add milk when reheating.

Tip: Eat small portions; excessive sweetness can trigger nausea.

Gentle Vegetable Broth with Noodles

⏱ Quick | 🍜 Gentle | 🌿 Plant-Based

Prep time: 5 minutes

Cook time: 12 minutes

Serves: 1

Why It Works

Clear broth hydrates, soft noodles offer easy-to-digest carbs. This simple soup is soothing and gentle for upset stomachs.

Ingredients

- 1½ cups low-sodium vegetable broth
- ½ cup rice noodles or thin pasta
- ¼ cup cooked carrots, diced small
- ¼ tsp salt
- ¼ tsp white pepper (optional)
- 1 tsp fresh parsley, chopped (optional)

Instructions

1. Boil broth, add noodles and cook per package directions.
2. Add carrots, heat through, and season with salt and pepper.

Nutrition (per serving)

- Calories: 180
- Protein: 4g
- Carbs: 38g
- Fat: 1g
- Fiber: 2g
- Sodium: 580mg

Substitutions

- Add tofu for more protein
- Use zucchini noodles for fewer carbs
- Swap carrots for spinach

Storage

Refrigerate up to 3 days. Add broth when reheating.

Tip: Sip broth first, then eat noodles slowly.

Key Takeaways

- Gentle meals focus on simple carbs, lean proteins, and minimal fats to combat nausea.
- Foods like white rice, toast, broth, and soft eggs are easier on the stomach than rich, spicy dishes.
- Maintaining protein intake is crucial; aim for 15–20g per meal if possible.
- Ingredients like ginger, miso, and bone broth naturally support digestion and hydration.
- Eat slowly and in small portions to prevent overwhelming your digestive system.
- Prepare and store recipes for quick access during nausea flare-ups.
- If nausea persists beyond dose escalation, consult your healthcare provider.
- Gentle meals are temporary solutions; return to balanced meals as symptoms improve.

Chapter 15:
High-Protein Smoothies & Liquid Nutrition

When appetite wanes on GLP-1 medication, consuming solid meals can be challenging. Smoothies offer an effective alternative, delivering essential protein and nutrients in a form that's easy to tolerate, even when nausea or early satiety occurs.

Liquid nutrition is not a long-term substitute for whole foods, but it helps meet protein needs on low-appetite days. Research supports an intake of 1–1.5 grams of protein per kilogram of body weight daily to preserve muscle mass during GLP-1 therapy. A well-crafted smoothie can provide 25–40 grams of protein per serving, which is often easier to consume than solid meats.

These recipes tackle common GLP-1 challenges: they're portion-controlled to prevent overfilling, balanced to avoid blood sugar spikes, and designed for digestive comfort. Each recipe includes dairy-free modifications and tips to mitigate nausea.

Use smoothies strategically—as meal replacements on low-appetite days, post-workout nutrition, or to ensure protein intake. Pair them with resistance training to maximize muscle preservation. The recipes range from quick breakfast blends to dessert-style options, prioritizing protein density, digestive tolerance, and blood sugar stability.

Classic Vanilla Protein Shake

Quick | High Protein | Gentle

Why It Works

This foundational recipe provides clean protein without overwhelming flavors that can trigger nausea. The combination of whey protein and Greek yogurt supplies complete amino acids for muscle preservation, while vanilla offers a mild taste. The banana adds natural sweetness and potassium without causing blood sugar spikes.

Ingredients

- 1 scoop vanilla whey protein isolate (25g protein)
- ½ cup plain Greek yogurt (12g protein)
- ½ medium banana, frozen
- 1 tablespoon almond butter
- ¾ cup unsweetened almond milk
- ½ teaspoon vanilla extract
- 3–4 ice cubes
- Optional: 1 teaspoon honey

Instructions

1. Add almond milk to the blender first.
2. Add Greek yogurt, protein powder, and almond butter.
3. Add frozen banana and ice cubes.
4. Blend on high for 45–60 seconds until smooth.
5. Adjust consistency with water if needed.
6. Consume within 30 minutes for optimal texture.

Nutrition (per serving)

- Calories: 385
- Protein: 40g
- Carbohydrates: 28g
- Fiber: 4g
- Fat: 12g
- Sugar: 16g

Prep time: 3 minutes

Cook time: 0 minutes

Substitutions

- **Dairy-free:** Use coconut yogurt and extra protein powder
- **Nut-free:** Use sunflower seed butter
- **Lower carb:** Use ¼ banana and add ¼ avocado

Storage Tips

Best consumed immediately. Refrigerate up to 4 hours; do not freeze.

GLP-1 Tips

Start with a half portion if experiencing nausea. Sip slowly over 20–30 minutes.

Berry Blast Antioxidant Smoothie

⏱ Quick | ◯ High Protein | 🌿 Plant-Based Option

Why It Works

Berries provide antioxidants and fiber with minimal sugar impact. The mix of plant and dairy proteins offers a complete amino acid profile, while flaxseed adds omega-3s and fiber for digestive support.

Ingredients

- 1 scoop vanilla or unflavored protein powder (20–25g protein)
- ½ cup plain Greek yogurt (12g protein)
- ¾ cup mixed frozen berries
- 1 tablespoon ground flaxseed
- 1 cup unsweetened almond milk
- ½ teaspoon lemon zest
- 5–6 ice cubes

Instructions

1. Combine almond milk and Greek yogurt in a blender.
2. Add protein powder and flaxseed; pulse briefly.
3. Add frozen berries, lemon zest, and ice.
4. Blend on high for 60 seconds until smooth.
5. Add mint leaves for extra flavor if desired.

Nutrition (per serving)

- Calories: 340
- Protein: 38g
- Carbohydrates: 25g
- Fiber: 7g
- Fat: 9g
- Sugar: 13g

Prep time: 4 minutes

Cook time: 0 minutes

Substitutions

- **Plant-based:** Use pea protein and coconut yogurt
- **Lower sugar:** Reduce berries; add cauliflower rice
- **Nut-free:** Use oat milk

Storage Tips

Consume fresh. Refrigerate up to 6 hours; shake if separated.

GLP-1 Tips

The fiber from berries moderates sugar absorption. Tart flavors may be more tolerable.

Chocolate Peanut Butter Power Shake

🕐 Quick | ◯ High Protein | 👫 Family Friendly

Why It Works

This indulgent smoothie makes protein intake enjoyable. Cocoa powder offers flavonoids for cardiovascular benefits, while whey and peanut butter sustain energy.

Ingredients

- 1 scoop chocolate whey protein isolate (25g protein)
- 2 tablespoons natural peanut butter (8g protein)
- 1 tablespoon unsweetened cocoa powder
- 1 cup unsweetened almond milk
- ½ medium banana, frozen
- 1 tablespoon chia seeds
- 4–5 ice cubes
- Pinch of sea salt

Instructions

1. Add almond milk to the blender.
2. Add peanut butter, protein powder, and cocoa powder.
3. Add banana, chia seeds, and salt.
4. Blend on high for 60–75 seconds until smooth.

Nutrition (per serving)

- Calories: 420
- Protein: 37g
- Carbohydrates: 30g
- Fiber: 9g
- Fat: 18g
- Sugar: 12g

Prep time: 4 minutes

Cook time: 0 minutes

Substitutions

- **Nut-free:** Use sunflower seed butter or tahini
- **Lower fat:** Reduce peanut butter; add PB2
- **Dairy-free:** Use plant-based protein

Storage Tips

Consume within 2 hours. Add water if thickened.

GLP-1 Tips

Consume slowly over 30 minutes. The chocolate flavor masks protein taste for some.

Tropical Green Machine

Why It Works

Leafy greens offer essential micronutrients, while tropical fruits provide an approachable flavor. Ginger aids digestive comfort.

Ingredients

- 1 scoop vanilla pea protein powder (20g protein)
- 1 cup fresh spinach, packed
- ½ cup frozen mango chunks
- ½ cup frozen pineapple chunks
- ½-inch fresh ginger, peeled
- 1 tablespoon hemp seeds (3g protein)
- 1 cup coconut water
- ½ cup unsweetened coconut milk
- Juice of ½ lime

Instructions

1. Add coconut water and milk to the blender.
2. Add spinach and ginger; blend briefly.
3. Add protein powder and hemp seeds.
4. Add mango, pineapple, and lime juice.
5. Blend on high for 60 seconds until smooth.

Nutrition (per serving)

- Calories: 355
- Protein: 26g
- Carbohydrates: 42g
- Fiber: 6g
- Fat: 9g
- Sugar: 28g

Prep time: 5 minutes

Cook time: 0 minutes

Substitutions

- **Lower sugar:** Reduce fruit; add cauliflower rice
- **Higher protein:** Add extra protein powder
- **Nut-free:** Already nut-free

Storage Tips

Drink within 4 hours. Freeze for a protein-rich treat.

GLP-1 Tips

Ginger aids nausea; the sweetness is gentle on sensitive stomachs.

Cinnamon Roll Breakfast Shake

⏱ Quick | ◯ High Protein | 🥣 Gentle | 👨‍👧 Family Friendly

Why It Works

This smoothie mimics comfort food while providing serious nutrition. Cinnamon supports blood sugar regulation, complementing GLP-1.

Ingredients

- 1 scoop vanilla whey protein isolate (25g protein)
- ⅓ cup plain Greek yogurt (8g protein)
- ¼ cup rolled oats
- 1 teaspoon ground cinnamon
- ½ teaspoon vanilla extract
- 1 tablespoon almond butter
- 1 cup unsweetened almond milk
- ½ teaspoon maple extract or syrup
- 5–6 ice cubes
- Pinch of nutmeg

Instructions

1. Soften oats in almond milk for 2 minutes.
2. Add Greek yogurt, protein powder, almond butter.
3. Add cinnamon, vanilla, maple extract, nutmeg.
4. Add ice cubes; blend on high for 75 seconds.

Nutrition (per serving)

- Calories: 395
- Protein: 38g
- Carbohydrates: 32g
- Fiber: 6g
- Fat: 12g
- Sugar: 8g

Prep time: 5 minutes (includes oat soaking)

Cook time: 0 minutes

Substitutions

- **Gluten-free:** Use certified gluten-free oats
- **Dairy-free:** Use plant-based protein, coconut yogurt
- **Lower carb:** Reduce oats; add chia seeds

Storage Tips

Consume within 3 hours. Add water to thin if needed.

GLP-1 Tips

The cinnamon roll flavor is comforting. Oats provide fiber without irritation.

Mocha Coffee Protein Smoothie

○ Quick | ○ High Protein

Why It Works

This energizing smoothie combines caffeine and protein, addressing fatigue. Cold brew coffee's smoother caffeine kick is gentler on the stomach.

Ingredients

- 1 scoop chocolate protein powder (25g protein)
- ¾ cup cold brew coffee
- ½ cup plain Greek yogurt (12g protein)
- 1 tablespoon unsweetened cocoa powder
- 1 tablespoon almond butter
- ¼ cup unsweetened almond milk
- 1 teaspoon vanilla extract
- 6–8 ice cubes

Instructions

1. Add coffee and almond milk to the blender.
2. Add Greek yogurt, protein powder, cocoa powder.
3. Add almond butter and vanilla.
4. Add ice cubes; blend on high for 45–60 seconds.

Nutrition (per serving)

- Calories: 360
- Protein: 40g
- Carbohydrates: 20g
- Fiber: 5g
- Fat: 12g
- Sugar: 8g

Prep time: 3 minutes

Cook time: 0 minutes

Substitutions

- **Decaf:** Use decaf coffee
- **Dairy-free:** Use coconut yogurt
- **Lower fat:** Use PB2

Storage Tips

Best consumed immediately. Refrigerate up to 4 hours.

GLP-1 Tips

Caffeine may increase nausea for some. Avoid on an empty stomach.

Creamy Avocado Lime Smoothie

🕐 Quick | ◯ High Protein | 🌿 Plant-Based | 🍵 Gentle

Why It Works

Avocado offers creaminess without dairy and provides healthy fats that support nutrient absorption. Lime adds brightness without irritating the stomach.

Ingredients

- 1 scoop unflavored or vanilla plant protein powder (20g protein)
- ½ medium ripe avocado
- 1 cup unsweetened almond milk
- ½ cup coconut water
- Juice of 1 lime
- 1 tablespoon hemp seeds (3g protein)
- 1 tablespoon honey or 2 dates
- ½ teaspoon vanilla extract
- 6–7 ice cubes

Instructions

1. Add almond milk and coconut water to the blender.
2. Add avocado, protein powder, hemp seeds.
3. Add lime juice, honey, vanilla extract.
4. Add ice cubes; blend on high for 60 seconds.

Nutrition (per serving)

- Calories: 380
- Protein: 25g
- Carbohydrates: 35g
- Fiber: 9g
- Fat: 16g
- Sugar: 20g

Prep time: 4 minutes

Cook time: 0 minutes

Substitutions

- **Lower carb:** Use stevia rather than honey
- **Nut-free:** Use oat milk
- **Higher protein:** Add silken tofu

Storage Tips

Consume within 2 hours. Add lime juice to slow oxidation.

GLP-1 Tips

The neutral flavor is ideal for severe nausea days. Sip slowly.

Pumpkin Spice Protein Shake

⏱ Quick | ◯ High Protein | 🍲 Gentle | 👨‍👩‍👧 Family Friendly

Why It Works

Pumpkin puree provides vitamin A, fiber, and a creamy base with minimal calories. Warming spices aid digestion and reduce nausea.

Ingredients

- 1 scoop vanilla whey protein isolate (25g protein)
- ½ cup pure pumpkin puree
- ½ cup plain Greek yogurt (12g protein)
- 1 cup unsweetened almond milk
- 1 teaspoon pumpkin pie spice
- ½ teaspoon vanilla extract
- 1 tablespoon almond butter
- 1 tablespoon maple syrup or 2 dates
- 4–5 ice cubes

Instructions

1. Add almond milk to the blender.
2. Add pumpkin puree, Greek yogurt, protein powder.
3. Add almond butter, spices, vanilla.
4. Add sweetener and ice cubes; blend on high for 60–75 seconds.

Nutrition (per serving)

- Calories: 400
- Protein: 40g
- Carbohydrates: 32g
- Fiber: 7g
- Fat: 12g
- Sugar: 18g

Prep time: 4 minutes

Cook time: 0 minutes

Substitutions

- **Dairy-free:** Use plant protein and coconut yogurt
- **Lower sugar:** Use stevia or monk fruit
- **Nut-free:** Use sunflower seed butter

Storage Tips

Refrigerate up to 8 hours. Can freeze in portions.

GLP-1 Tips

The thick texture and warming spices reduce nausea. Increase spice if needed.

Blueberry Almond Protein Smoothie

⏱ Quick | ◯ High Protein | 🥣 Gentle

Why It Works

Blueberries provide antioxidants that support metabolic health. The combination of almond butter and protein offers sustained energy release.

Ingredients

- 1 scoop vanilla whey protein isolate (25g protein)
- 1 cup frozen blueberries
- 2 tablespoons almond butter (7g prothein)
- ½ cup plain Greek yogurt (12g protein)
- 1 cup unsweetened almond milk
- 1 tablespoon ground flaxseed
- ½ teaspoon almond extract
- 3–4 ice cubes

Instructions

1. Add almond milk to the blender.
2. Add Greek yogurt, protein powder, almond butter.
3. Add blueberries, flaxseed, almond extract, ice cubes.
4. Blend on high for 60 seconds.

Nutrition (per serving)

- Calories: 485
- Protein: 45g
- Carbohydrates: 33g
- Fiber: 8g
- Fat: 19g
- Sugar: 19g

Prep time: 3 minutes

Cook time: 0 minutes

Substitutions

- **Lower fat:** Reduce almond butter; add protein
- **Nut-free:** Use sunflower seed butter
- **Plant-based:** Use pea protein, coconut yogurt

Storage Tips

Consume within 6 hours. Freeze in ice cube trays for future use.

GLP-1 Tips

Ideal post-training or as a meal replacement. Consume slowly.

Strawberry Banana Collagen Boost

⏱ Quick | ◯ High Protein | 👫 Family Friendly | 🍲 Gentle

Why It Works

Collagen peptides support skin, joint, and gut health. The classic strawberry-banana combination is gentle on sensitive stomachs.

Ingredients

- 1 scoop vanilla whey protein isolate (25g protein)
- 2 scoops unflavored collagen peptides (20g protein)
- 1 cup frozen strawberries
- ½ medium banana, frozen
- ½ cup plain Greek yogurt (12g protein)
- 1 cup unsweetened almond milk
- 1 tablespoon chia seeds
- ½ teaspoon vanilla extract
- 3–4 ice cubes

Instructions

1. Add almond milk to the blender.
2. Add Greek yogurt, whey protein, collagen peptides.
3. Add strawberries, banana, chia seeds, vanilla.
4. Blend on high for 75 seconds.

Nutrition (per serving)

- Calories: 450
- Protein: 57g
- Carbohydrates: 35g
- Fiber: 8g
- Fat: 8g
- Sugar: 20g

Prep time: 4 minutes

Cook time: 0 minutes

Substitutions

- **Dairy-free:** Use plant protein and coconut yogurt
- **Lower protein:** Omit collagen peptides
- **Berry variation:** Use mixed berries

Storage Tips

Best consumed within 4 hours. Chia seeds thicken over time.

GLP-1 Tips

The high protein content is ideal for one protein-rich meal. Gentle on digestion.

Key Takeaways

- **Liquid nutrition provides essential protein when solid food feels impossible**—smoothies deliver 25–57g protein per serving, meeting daily needs even with suppressed appetite.
- **Protein-to-carb ratios prevent blood sugar spikes**—combining protein, healthy fats, and fiber slows sugar absorption, avoiding the crashes that worsen GLP-1 side effects.
- **Texture matters for tolerability**—smooth, creamy consistency requires less digestive effort than solid food, making smoothies ideal for nausea days.
- **Strategic ingredient choices support muscle preservation**—complete protein sources (whey, Greek yogurt, plant protein blends) provide amino acids needed during weight loss.
- **Ginger, cinnamon, and mild flavors reduce nausea triggers**—avoid overly sweet or strong flavors when experiencing GI symptoms.
- **Consume slowly over 20–40 minutes**—sipping prevents overwhelming your already-slowed digestive system and reduces discomfort.

- **Use smoothies as meal replacements, not additions**—these recipes contain 340–485 calories and are designed to replace, not supplement, meals.

- **Dairy-free options maintain protein density**—plant-based proteins, coconut yogurt, and nut butters provide complete nutrition without dairy.

PART 5
TROUBLESHOOTING & REAL-LIFE SCENARIOS

Chapter 16:
If You Feel Too Full

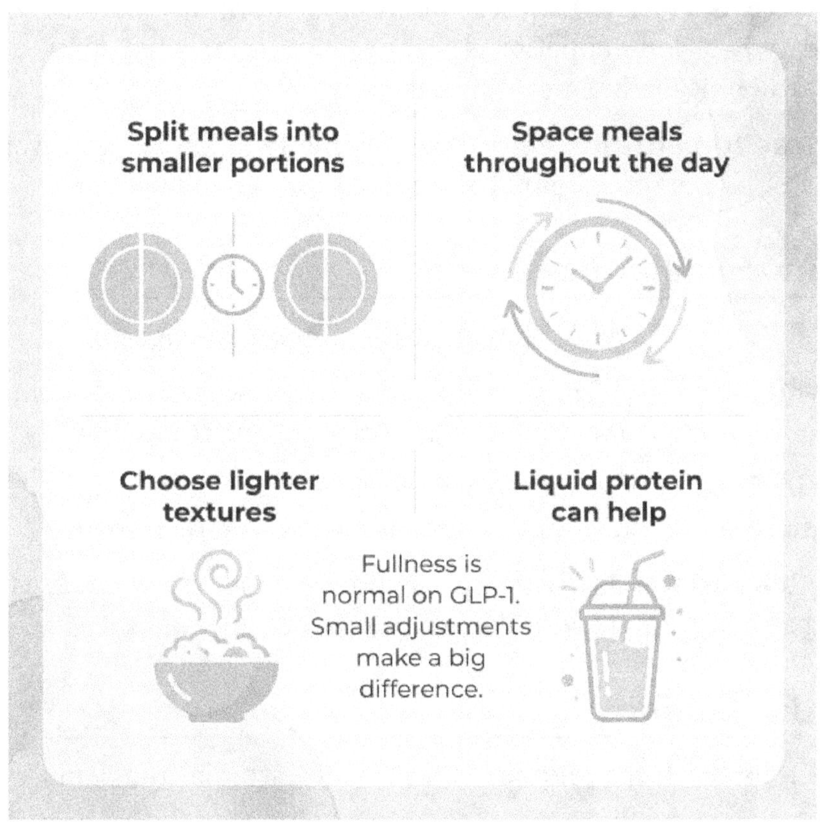

Feeling uncomfortably full while on GLP-1 medication is common - it's not solely about eating less. The medication slows gastric emptying, meaning food remains in your stomach longer. This can make even small portions feel overwhelming. The challenge is managing fullness while ensuring enough protein and nutrients to preserve muscle mass. This chapter provides practical strategies to navigate persistent fullness without compromising nutrition.

Why Fullness Becomes a Problem

GLP-1 medications reduce hunger by slowing down stomach processing. This delayed emptying extends feelings of fullness for hours after a modest meal. For some, it leads to skipping meals, risking muscle loss and nutrient deficiencies.

This concern is heightened by significant weight loss, including lean muscle mass. When fullness prevents adequate protein intake, muscle preservation becomes more difficult.

Adjust Portion Timing

If standard meal timing results in discomfort, consider these adjustments:

Eat smaller amounts more frequently. Instead of three meals, try five to six mini-meals throughout the day. This helps your stomach manage food without being overloaded.

Front-load protein early in the day. Many find morning tolerance higher. Prioritize protein-rich foods when your appetite is strongest, even if it requires a non-traditional breakfast like leftover chicken or a protein shake.

Avoid eating close to bedtime. Lying down with a full stomach can worsen discomfort. Finish eating at least two to three hours before sleep.

Split Meals Into Smaller Portions

Breaking meals into smaller servings can make them more manageable:

Divide a single meal in half. Consume the first portion, wait 60 to 90 minutes, then finish. This prevents overwhelming your stomach while meeting nutritional needs.

Focus on protein first. In each split meal, prioritize high-protein foods. If only half a plate can be finished, make sure it includes chicken, fish, eggs, or Greek yogurt.

Use smaller plates and bowls. Visual cues matter. A smaller plate with a full portion looks more satisfying than a large plate with the same amount.

Liquid Nutrition Options

When solid food feels too heavy, liquids can provide essential nutrients without excessive fullness:

Protein shakes or smoothies. Blend protein powder with milk, Greek yogurt, or a banana for a nutrient-dense option. Aim for 20 to 30 grams of protein per shake.

Bone broth or protein-enriched soups. Warm liquids are often better tolerated. Add collagen powder or shredded chicken to boost protein content.

Avoid empty-calorie liquids. Juice, soda, and sugary drinks occupy stomach space without offering protein or nutrients. Stick to options supporting muscle preservation.

Common Mistakes

- **Skipping meals entirely.** Prolonged gaps increase muscle breakdown and nutrient deficiencies.
- **Relying only on liquids long-term.** Shakes can lack the fiber and micronutrients of whole foods.
- **Forcing large portions.** Overeating can worsen nausea and create negative food associations.

- **Ignoring hydration.** Dehydration worsens fullness and discomfort. Sip water throughout the day, separate from meals.

Key Takeaways

- GLP-1 medications slow gastric emptying, making fullness last longer.
- Eating smaller, more frequent meals helps maintain nutrient intake.
- Front-load protein early when appetite is stronger.
- Split larger meals into two portions separated by 60 to 90 minutes.
- Use protein shakes, smoothies, and enriched soups when solid food is too heavy.
- Avoid skipping meals—prolonged gaps increase muscle loss risk.
- Prioritize protein in every session, even if portions are small.

Chapter 17:
If You're Losing Weight Too Fast

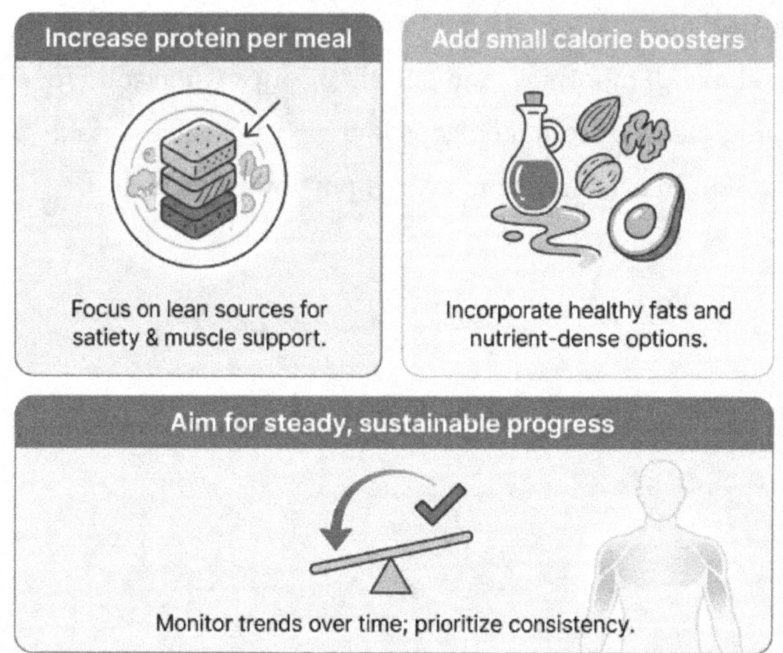

Rapid weight loss might at first seem like a success, but it carries hidden risks. When you're shedding pounds faster than anticipated on GLP-1 medication, you're likely losing more muscle than desirable. This chapter explores what happens when the scale moves too quickly and how to slow the process while safeguarding your lean tissue.

Fast weight loss isn't just an aesthetic issue. Excessive muscle loss can weaken your metabolism, reduce strength, and leave you feeling fatigued. The goal is controlled, sustainable fat loss - not a race to the lowest number.

Why Fast Weight Loss Is a Problem

GLP-1 medications work by reducing appetite and slowing digestion. When appetite diminishes sharply, many people unintentionally under-eat. This creates a larger calorie deficit than intended, leading to rapid weight loss from both fat and muscle stores.

Muscle tissue needs energy to maintain. When your body senses severe calorie restriction, it breaks down muscle for fuel. This is particularly problematic for older adults and females, who face a higher risk of muscle loss during weight reduction.

The result: you lose weight quickly, but a significant portion comes from lean mass rather than fat. Over time, this slows your metabolism and complicates long-term weight maintenance.

Increase Protein Density

To slow excessive weight loss, increase protein density in every meal. This doesn't mean eating more volume; it means selecting foods with higher protein per bite.

Focus on compact, protein-rich options:

- Greek yogurt instead of regular yogurt
- Cottage cheese over cream cheese
- Lean ground beef or turkey in smaller portions
- Eggs prepared in various forms
- Protein shakes when solid food feels difficult
- Canned tuna or salmon for quick meals

Since GLP-1 medications reduce appetite, you might manage only small portions. Make every bite count by prioritizing protein. Aim to consume protein-rich meals within 30 to 60 minutes after resistance training to maximize muscle recovery.

If meeting protein targets through whole foods is challenging, consider a high-quality protein supplement. Choose options that are easy to digest and don't worsen nausea.

Add Gentle Calorie Boosters

Slowing weight loss requires adding calories without overwhelming your reduced appetite. The key is choosing nutrient-dense, calorie-rich foods in small amounts.

Effective calorie boosters:

- Nut butters (almond, peanut, cashew)
- Avocado slices or guacamole
- Olive oil drizzled on vegetables or salads
- Full-fat dairy products
- Nuts and seeds as snacks
- Cheese in moderate portions

These foods provide concentrated energy without requiring large portions. A tablespoon of almond butter adds about 100 calories. A quarter avocado contributes healthy fats and about 60 calories. Small additions throughout the day can significantly slow weight loss without causing discomfort.

Avoid processed or sugary foods to increase calories. While they're calorie-dense, they don't support muscle preservation or overall health.

Monitor Your Rate of Loss

Track your weight weekly, not daily. Aim for a loss rate of 1 to 2 pounds per week. If you're consistently losing more than 2 pounds weekly, your deficit is too aggressive.

Adjust your intake gradually. Add one calorie booster at a time and reassess after a week. This prevents overcorrection and helps you find the right balance.

Common Mistakes

- **Ignoring protein targets** – Protein is crucial when weight loss accelerates.
- **Skipping meals due to low appetite** – Eating small, frequent meals maintains intake.
- **Focusing only on the scale** – Muscle loss won't always show on the scale.
- **Avoiding resistance training** – Strength training is essential to preserve muscle.
- **Adding empty calories** – Choose nutrient-dense options, not junk food.

Key Takeaways

- Rapid weight loss on GLP-1 medication often indicates excessive muscle loss.
- Increase protein density by choosing compact, high-protein foods at each meal.
- Add gentle calorie boosters like nut butters, avocado, and olive oil to slow weight loss.
- Consume protein within 30 to 60 minutes post-exercise for optimal muscle recovery.
- Monitor your rate of loss weekly and adjust intake if losing more than 2 pounds per week.
- Combine higher protein intake with resistance training to protect lean mass.
- Avoid relying on processed foods to increase calories—choose nutrient-dense options.

Chapter 18:
If Weight Loss Stalls

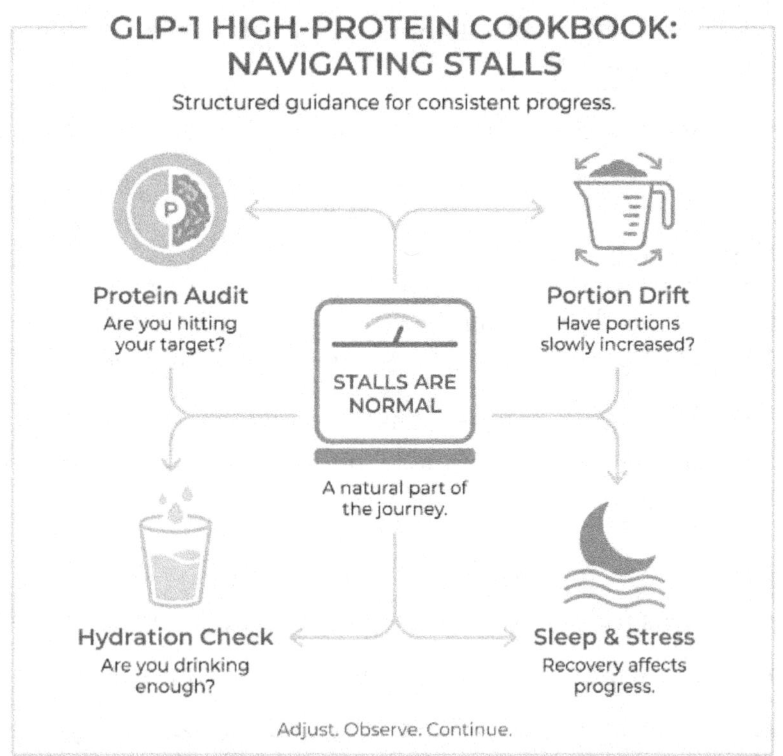

Weight loss plateaus can be both normal and frustrating. After experiencing weeks or months of progress on GLP-1 medication, the scale may suddenly stop moving. This doesn't necessarily mean the medication is ineffective or that you've made mistakes. Instead, it often indicates that your body has adapted, and unnoticed changes in habits may have occurred. Fortunately, most stalls can be addressed by auditing several key areas. This chapter guides you through common culprits and how to troubleshoot them systematically.

Run a Protein Audit

Appetite suppression can lead to unintentionally low protein intake. Initially, you may have focused on meeting your protein targets, but over time, portions can shrink, meals might be skipped, and protein intake can quietly decrease.

Low protein intake not only slows fat loss but also accelerates muscle loss. Research indicates that GLP-1 users may have a higher risk of reduced protein consumption due to appetite changes. As muscle mass declines, so does metabolic rate, potentially contributing to a plateau.

What to Do:

- Track your protein intake for three days using an app or notebook.
- Compare your average to your target (typically 0.7–1.0 grams per pound of goal body weight).
- If you're falling short, prioritize protein at every meal before adding other foods.
- Focus on high-protein, low-volume options: Greek yogurt, cottage cheese, eggs, lean poultry, fish, and protein shakes.

If nausea or fullness limits intake, try smaller, more frequent protein servings instead of large meals.

Check for Portion Drift

Portion sizes can creep upward over time, even with appetite suppression. Habitual eating, social settings, and visual cues may lead to larger servings than necessary.

This is particularly common with calorie-dense foods such as nuts, oils, nut butters, and cheese. A tablespoon can become two, and a handful can turn into a cup. These small increases accumulate rapidly.

What to Do:

- Re-measure portions for one week, especially fats and carbohydrates.
- Use a food scale or measuring cups to reset your visual portion sense.
- Pay attention to condiments, cooking oils, and snacks - they often harbor hidden calories.
- When dining out, consider that restaurant portions are often 2–3 times larger than home-cooked meals.

Portion drift is a natural behavioral shift that's easily corrected once identified.

Reassess Hydration

Dehydration can mimic hunger, slow digestion, and reduce energy expenditure. GLP-1 medications slow gastric emptying, and inadequate hydration worsens this effect. Low water intake also raises the risk of constipation and fatigue, indirectly stalling progress.

Some users drink less because they feel less thirsty or consume fewer water-rich foods.

What to Do:

- Aim for at least 64–80 ounces of water daily, more if you're active or in a hot climate.
- Start your day with 16 ounces of water before eating.
- Set hourly reminders if you frequently forget to drink.

- Herbal teas, sparkling water, and water-rich foods (cucumbers, melons, broths) all count.

While hydration alone won't break a plateau, it supports digestion, energy, and adherence to other habits.

Evaluate Sleep and Stress

Poor sleep and chronic stress interfere with weight loss through hormonal pathways. Sleep deprivation increases ghrelin (the hunger hormone) and decreases leptin (the satiety hormone), even with GLP-1 medication. Stress elevates cortisol, promoting fat retention - especially around the midsection - and can increase cravings for high-calorie comfort foods.

If your sleep or stress levels have worsened since starting GLP-1 therapy, this may contribute to your stall.

What to Do:

- Aim for 7–9 hours of sleep per night.
- Establish a consistent bedtime routine and limit screen time before bed.
- Identify and address major stressors where possible.
- Incorporate daily stress management: walking, breathing exercises, journaling, or meditation.
- Avoid relying on food as a primary coping mechanism for stress.

Perfect sleep or zero stress isn't necessary for weight loss, but significant deficits in either area can noticeably slow progress.

Key Takeaways

- Weight loss plateaus are common and typically reversible with targeted adjustments.
- Protein intake often declines over time due to appetite suppression—track and address it.
- Portion drift occurs gradually; re-measure foods to reset portion awareness.
- Hydration supports digestion, energy, and overall adherence—ensure adequate intake.
- Poor sleep and high stress disrupt hunger hormones and fat metabolism, even with GLP-1 medication.
- Tackle one variable at a time and allow each change 1–2 weeks before introducing another.
- Most stalls resolve with small, consistent corrections—not drastic overhauls.

Chapter 19:
Eating Out & Traveling on GLP-1

Restaurant meals and travel don't have to derail your progress while on GLP-1 medication. The challenge lies in navigating oversized portions, limited protein options, and unpredictable meal timing when your appetite is already suppressed.

Many on GLP-1s either force down food they don't want or skip meals altogether, which can accelerate muscle loss. This chapter provides practical strategies to maintain your protein intake and protect muscle mass while eating away from home.

The Restaurant Challenge on GLP-1

GLP-1 medications slow gastric emptying and create intense fullness signals. In restaurants, this leads to a problem: portions are often 2-3 times what you can comfortably eat. This results in wasted food or the uncomfortable feeling of eating past satiety.

Another issue is meal composition. Restaurant entrees typically emphasize starches and fats over protein. When you can only eat a fraction of what's served, you risk missing your protein target.

Since up to 20-30% of weight loss on GLP-1s can come from muscle mass, every meal matters. Avoiding protein shortfalls adds up quickly, especially when you frequently eat out or travel.

Restaurant Ordering Strategy

Lead with protein. Choose your entrée based on the protein source, then modify everything else. Opt for grilled chicken, fish, steak, or shrimp as the focus. Ask for double protein if needed—most places accommodate this for a small charge.

Plan for leftovers. Before your meal arrives, request a to-go container. When served, portion out half for later. This removes pressure to finish and provides a ready-made, protein-rich meal for the next day.

Replace, don't add. Rather than adding sides, replace standard starches. Swap fries for grilled chicken. Replace pasta with extra vegetables and a salmon filet. You're not eating more—just shifting your focus to protein.

Use appetizers strategically. Opt for protein-forward appetizers like shrimp cocktail, chicken skewers, or tuna tartare as your main course. These are often better portioned and higher in protein than traditional entrées.

Portion Control Without Waste

The one-third rule. Plan to eat about one-third of a standard restaurant portion. This aligns with the reduced capacity experienced on GLP-1s. Knowing this removes guilt and helps you order appropriately.

Share strategically. Share an entrée with a companion, but add a protein-rich appetizer or side for yourself. This way, you prioritize protein within a reasonable portion.

Order from lunch menus. Lunch portions are generally 20-30% smaller than dinner ones but have similar protein content, making them ideal for evening dining.

Airport and Travel Survival Plan

Pack protein insurance. TSA permits solid protein foods through security. Bring jerky, hard-boiled eggs, cheese sticks, or protein bars. These act as backups when delays or limited options threaten your intake.

Pre-flight protein loading. Eat a protein-rich meal before heading to the airport. You may not feel hungry for hours, but having protein on board prevents hunger when only pretzels are available.

Airport restaurant priorities. Look for:

- Grilled chicken salads (request double chicken)
- Breakfast spots with all-day eggs
- Poke bowls or sushi (focus on fish, minimize rice)
- Burrito bowls (skip tortilla and rice, double protein)

Hotel room essentials. Request a room with a fridge. Stock it with:

- Greek yogurt cups
- Pre-cooked rotisserie chicken
- String cheese
- Ready-to-drink protein shakes

This creates a protein safety net for mornings or evenings with limited restaurant options.

Timing flexibility.

GLP-1s reduce hunger cues, leading to potential meal skipping during travel. Set phone reminders for meal times. Even without hunger, maintaining protein intake is vital to protect muscle mass.

Common Mistakes When Eating Out

- **Saving appetite for one big meal.** This can result in lower total protein intake than spreading it throughout the day.
- **Ordering based on taste.** Choose based on protein content first.
- **Drinking calories before eating.** Alcohol and sugary drinks fill space without providing protein.
- **Assuming small portions mean less protein.** You need the same amount of protein in less total food—prioritize density.
- **Skipping meals during travel.** Missing meals equates to missing protein, which accelerates muscle loss over time.

Quick Takeaways

- Order restaurant meals based on protein source and modify sides
- Plan for leftovers by portioning half before eating
- Use the one-third rule for portion control
- Pack solid protein foods for travel as a backup
- Eat a protein-rich meal before airport travel
- Request hotel fridges and stock with ready-to-eat proteins
- Set meal time reminders during travel - reduced hunger doesn't mean reduced protein needs
- Opt for lunch menus or appetizers for portions aligned with GLP-1 appetite

Chapter 20:

Cooking for Someone on GLP-1

When someone you care about starts GLP-1 medication, mealtimes can evolve. Your partner, who once finished every bite, may now eat only a fraction. Your spouse might love your lasagna but can't manage more than a few bites. This isn't a critique of your cooking - it's the medication at work.

GLP-1s can reduce appetite by up to 40% and slow digestion, making the person on medication feel full more quickly and stay full longer. For family members who cook, this creates a challenge: how do you prepare meals that satisfy everyone without making two different dinners every night?

This chapter offers practical strategies to cook meals that accommodate both GLP-1 users and the rest of your household. You'll learn to adjust portions, enhance protein intake, and create flexible dishes that cater to differing appetites at the same table.

Understanding the Challenge

The person on GLP-1 isn't being choosy; their body is responding to hormonal signals that suppress hunger and create early fullness. What once was a normal portion now feels overwhelming. Former favorite foods may suddenly become unappealing or sit heavily in their stomach.

This can create tension at mealtimes. You don't want to waste food or cook twice, and you certainly don't want the person on medication to feel isolated or guilty for not eating.

The solution is strategic meal design that allows customization at the table - not separate meals.

The Build-Your-Plate Approach

The most effective strategy for mixed households is component-based cooking. Rather than serving pre-plated meals or casseroles, prepare meal elements separately to allow everyone to combine them as needed.

Basic framework:

- Lean protein (grilled chicken, fish, lean beef, tofu)
- Non-starchy vegetables (roasted broccoli, sautéed greens, salad)
- Starchy side (rice, potatoes, pasta, bread)
- Optional additions (cheese, sauces, nuts)

Family members not on medication can load their plates normally. The GLP-1 user takes a smaller portion, focuses on protein, and adds vegetables as tolerated.

This approach removes the need for duplicate cooking while giving everyone control over their portions.

Portion Adjustments That Work

When plating for someone on GLP-1, think in quarters, not halves.

A standard dinner might be 6 ounces of protein, 1 cup of vegetables, and 1 cup of starch. For the GLP-1 user, start with 3–4 ounces of protein, ½ cup of vegetables, and a small amount of starch if desired.

Use smaller plates or bowls. A smaller visual portion on a smaller plate appears more satisfying than a tiny amount on a large plate.

Serve meals family-style when possible. Put serving dishes on the table and let everyone plate their own food. This removes pressure and allows the person on medication to take what feels manageable without explanation.

Protein Add-Ons Without Extra Cooking

The GLP-1 user needs to prioritize protein to preserve muscle mass, but they're eating less overall. Every bite counts.

Ways to boost protein without separate meals:

- Add a hard-boiled egg to their salad
- Sprinkle cottage cheese on their vegetables
- Offer Greek yogurt as a side instead of sour cream
- Keep rotisserie chicken for quick protein additions
- Add a scoop of unflavored protein powder to soups or mashed potatoes
- Top their portion with an extra ounce of the main protein

These additions are quick and don't require separate preparation.

Shared Meals That Flex

Certain meal types naturally accommodate different portion needs without extra work.

Tacos or burrito bowls: Everyone builds their own. The GLP-1 user can skip the tortilla, use less rice, and load up on lean protein and vegetables.

Stir-fries: Serve protein and vegetables over rice for the family. The GLP-1 user takes mostly protein and vegetables with minimal rice.

Grilled proteins with sides: Grill chicken breasts or fish for everyone. Serve with roasted vegetables and a grain. Everyone customizes their plate.

Soups and stews: Make protein-forward versions with beans, chicken, or beef. Serve with bread on the side. The GLP-1 user can have a smaller bowl and skip the bread.

Pasta dishes: Cook pasta separately from the protein and sauce. The GLP-1 user can have more sauce and protein with a small amount of pasta, while others load up on noodles.

The key is separating components so portions can be individualized.

Managing Leftovers

Smaller portions mean more leftovers. Plan for this.

Cook the usual amount and expect the GLP-1 user to eat less. Pack leftovers immediately into single-serving containers as ready-made meals for lunches or future dinners.

If reheated food is a struggle, freeze individual portions for later when appetite may improve.

Common Mistakes Family Members Make

Pressuring them to eat more: Comments like "just a few more bites" create guilt and stress. Trust their fullness signals.

Making them feel wasteful: Smaller portions aren't wasteful if you plan for leftovers.

Cooking only their preferences: The whole family doesn't need to eat "diet food." Use the component approach to satisfy everyone.

Assuming they'll never eat certain foods again: Preferences can change on GLP-1, but they're not permanent. What doesn't work now might be fine later.

Skipping protein because they're not hungry: Even with reduced appetite, protein is a priority - offer it first.

When Appetite Is Especially Low

Some days, even small portions feel like too much. On these days, focus on nutrient density over volume.

Offer a protein shake made with Greek yogurt and protein powder. Serve a small bowl of chicken soup. Make a smoothie with protein, fruit, and spinach. Provide a cheese stick and berries.

The goal isn't a full meal - it's adequate protein and nutrition to prevent deficiency.

Key Takeaways

- Use component-based cooking so everyone customizes their plate
- Start GLP-1 users with quarter portions, not half portions
- Prioritize protein, then vegetables, then starches
- Add simple protein boosters like hard-boiled eggs or extra servings of protein
- Choose flexible meal formats like tacos, stir-fries, and build-your-own bowls
- Plan for leftovers instead of reducing cooking volume
- Never pressure someone on GLP-1 to eat more than feels comfortable
- On low-appetite days, focus on protein-rich, nutrient-dense small portions rather than full meals

Chapter 21:

Final Words

Eating well on GLP-1 medication is not complicated in principle. It requires protein at most meals, consistent structure, and realistic expectations. That is the foundation this book was built on.

What makes it challenging in practice is the disruption the medication creates. Appetite becomes unreliable. Meals that once felt routine now require effort. Foods that worked before may no longer sit well. These are physiological realities, not personal failures.

Progress in this context does not look like a linear march toward a goal.

It looks like eating adequately on the days when food feels unappealing. It looks like returning to structure after a week that went sideways. It looks like making a reasonable choice with what is available rather than waiting for the ideal conditions. That kind of incremental consistency is what this book was designed to support.

Protein as Muscle Protection

Muscle loss during weight loss on GLP-1 medication is not inevitable, but it is a real risk if protein intake is insufficient. The body requires amino acids to maintain lean tissue, and when calorie intake drops significantly, dietary protein becomes the primary line of defense.

This is why protein targets matter. Not as a performance metric, but as a physiological floor. Meeting your daily protein range on most days is one of the most direct things you can do to protect muscle mass and support physical function over time.

The meals in this book were designed with that floor in mind. High protein density per calorie. Soft textures when needed. Reasonable portion sizes that account for reduced appetite without abandoning nutritional adequacy.

Structure Reduces Overwhelm

Decision fatigue is real, and it is amplified when appetite is suppressed and nausea is a possibility. Having a default structure for meals, a short list of reliable proteins, and a backup plan for low-appetite days removes the need to make those decisions in the moment.

Structure is not rigidity. It is a framework that holds when motivation is low and conditions are imperfect. The meal templates, the emergency protein options, and the weekly planning tools in this book exist for exactly those moments.

Use them. Adapt them. Return to them when things drift.

GLP-1 Is a Tool, Not a Solution

GLP-1 receptor agonists are effective medications. The evidence for their impact on appetite regulation and metabolic health is substantial. They are also not complete in themselves.

Medication reduces appetite. It does not determine what you eat when you do eat.

It does not preserve muscle mass. It does not build sustainable habits or ensure nutritional adequacy. Those outcomes depend on the choices made within the window the medication creates. This book was written to help you use that window well.

Sustainability Over Extremes

Approaches that are very restrictive tend not to last. On GLP-1 medication, where appetite is already reduced, extreme restriction can accelerate muscle loss, disrupt energy levels, and make nutritional adequacy nearly impossible.

The goal is not to eat as little as possible. The goal is to eat enough of the right things, consistently, over time. That requires a level of flexibility and self-knowledge that rigid plans rarely support.

Small, consistent actions compound. Hitting 80 percent of your protein target most days is more valuable than perfect adherence for two weeks followed by a collapse. Sustainability is not a secondary concern. It is the actual goal.

Work with what you have. Build habits that can survive real life. Adjust without abandoning the framework entirely.

That is enough. That is, in fact, the whole thing.

What To Do Next

Start here. Keep it simple.

- Set your daily protein target. Based on your current body weight and activity level, identify the protein range that applies to you (from Chapter 2). Write it down. Post it somewhere visible. This number becomes your anchor for every meal decision.

- Follow the weekly meal structure for the next two weeks. Use the stabilization framework from Chapter 5 as your default. Do not try to optimize everything at once. Choose three or four reliable high-protein meals from the recipe section and rotate them. Reduce decisions, reduce friction.

- Prepare your low-appetite fallback list. Identify five to six high-protein options you can rely on when nausea or suppressed appetite make cooking difficult. These should require minimal preparation and be soft or liquid-based where possible. Keep the ingredients stocked. When appetite drops, you will not have to think about what to eat.

A Note on Medical Guidance

The information in this book is educational and is not a substitute for personalized medical advice. GLP-1 medications affect individuals differently, and nutritional needs vary based on age, body composition, health status, activity level, and the specific medication and dose you are using.

Work with your prescribing physician, a registered dietitian, or another qualified healthcare provider to establish protein targets and monitor your progress over time. Tracking strength, energy, and physical function alongside weight gives a more complete picture of how the medication and your nutrition plan are working together.

If you experience significant side effects, unexplained fatigue, or noticeable muscle weakness, bring these to your provider's attention. Adjustments to dose, timing, or nutritional strategy may be appropriate.

If This Book Was Helpful

If the structure, recipes, or approach here made your experience with GLP-1 medication a little easier to navigate, leaving a review would be genuinely useful.

Many people starting these medications feel uncertain about how to eat well while appetite is suppressed, and what they hear from others who have been in that position carries real weight.

An honest review, even a short one, can help someone at the beginning of this process feel less overwhelmed. When you have a moment, your perspective is worth sharing.